Quit SMOKING for GOOD

A Supportive Program for Permanent Smoking Cessation

by Andrea Baer

D1112918

THE CROSSING PRESS
FREEDOM, CALIFORNIA

Copyright © 1998 by Andrea Baer
Cover design by Victoria May
Cover photographs by Chip Simons/FPG Int., and Tom Campbell/FPG Int.
Interior design by Magnolia Studio
Printed in the U.S.A.

For information on bulk purchases or group discounts for this and other Crossing Press titles, please contact our Special Sales Manager at 800-777-1048.

Visit our Web site on the Internet: www.crossingpress.com

Disclaimer:
The ideas, suggestions, and techniques in this book are not intended to be a substitute for professional mental health care. Anyone with a history of serious mental illness should consult a licensed therapist or psychiatrist.

Library of Congress Cataloging-in-Publication Data

Baer, Andrea.
    Quit smoking for good : a supportive program for permanent
smoking cessation / by Andrea Baer
        p. cm. -- (Personal power)
    Includes bibliographical references.
    ISBN 0-89594-943-1 (pbk.)
    1. Smoking cessation programs. 2. Cigarette habit--Prevention.
3. Cigarette habit--Treatment. 4. Behavior therapy. I. Title.
II. Series.
RC567.B27   1998
613.85--dc21

                                                            98-24697
                                                                CIP

Contents

Preface

I'd rather die young than live without cigarettes, I thought, and I stopped crying as soon as I put a cigarette in my mouth. And, well, I knew I could always try stopping some other time.

Cigarettes were an integral part of my life for fifteen years, ever since junior high school. While other girls combed the malls looking for bargains, my best friend and I scanned the banks of a nearby lake, looking for washed-up cigarette butts. Doll dishes served as ashtrays to supply a tea party atmosphere. These after-school activities prepared me for college, where, due to limited funds, I again rolled my own.

I always had a vague sense that something was missing if I didn't have a cigarette smoldering nearby. If the guy I was dating complained about my chain-smoking, I would do us both a favor and dump him. Nothing could interfere with my two-pack-a-day habit, even severe flu.

The same compulsive personality that bolstered my smoking habit fueled my many repeated attempts to quit. Besides reading all the books on quitting, including the one that excited me the most—*How to Keep Smoking and Live*—I tried acupuncture, aversion therapy, hypnosis, and smoking cessation clinics, all with no lasting results. I became such hell to be around when I quit smoking even my friends who had encouraged me to quit would urge me for God's sake to continue smoking.

I tried cheating with Tiparillos, but once I started to chain-smoke them, I got migraine headaches every day. When I switched to clove cigarettes, they too had the same effect.

I have sincerely looked forward to and enjoyed almost every cigarette I have ever smoked. In fact, I couldn't even imagine life without cigarettes. I never thought that I could do absolutely nothing with my hands or my mouth. I never thought I would be able to drink coffee or alcohol or have a meal or sex without craving a cigarette. I never thought I would enjoy nonsmoking more than I enjoyed smoking.

Until I finally quit for good. And it was so painless it was anti-climactic because I had prepared myself for a battle. It had taken over fifty tries before I finally quit, and stumbled upon this program in the process. I then supplemented the program with interviews from ex-smokers and studies on the psychology of addiction in general.

This program can also help tobacco chewers. Smokeless tobacco, also known as snuff, can, like cigarettes cause health problems. An estimated one million people, mostly young adult males, use snuff, half of them on a regular basis.

Chewing tobacco contains more nicotine than cigarettes. It is buffered to facilitate its absorption through the mucous membranes. When mixing cigarettes and smokeless tobacco, nicotine levels sky-rocket.

Snuff users are more prone to throat, mouth, and stomach cancers, dental cavities, periodontal disease, mouth sores, and accelerated heart beat. And because of its high salt content, snuff is a factor in high blood pressure.

Many cancer specialists say cancer of the mouth is the worst cancer, because it spreads to other parts of the mouth and face, affecting how a person looks, breathes, tastes, and talks. Moreover, if not caught early, it can be very difficult to treat.

If you chew tobacco, try the program in this book in combination with some type of nicotine replacement therapy (see page 29).

Introduction

It can be discouraging to hear that only 2.5 percent of all smokers who try to quit actually do. Most of the programs out there simply don't work.

It's not that difficult to quit smoking for 72 hours. The problem is *staying* off cigarettes. This program provides the necessary mental preparation for quitting. It takes into account data from recent findings that show that most smokers rarely quit on their first attempt.

WHY THIS PROGRAM IS EFFECTIVE

This method emphasizes getting you off cigarettes with as little stress as possible. Here is what it will do for you.

Many smokers can't even picture themselves handling life without lighting up.

Since you have used cigarettes to insulate yourself from your emotions for so long, the program will help you adopt new coping skills, problem-solving strategies, and stress management tactics.

It takes practice to do anything right.

This program uses an assortment of exercises, addressing every possible smoking trigger with an arsenal of oral, behavioral, and mental substitutes. It also includes a rehearsal day before the actual quit date.

People smoke for different reasons in different situations.

For this reason, any effective cessation program must be specifically tailored to your particular smoking style.

It is a longer-than-usual program.

The length of the program is sixty days, which gives the smoker time to unlearn something that has generally taken years to learn. This extensive preparation also helps to prevent relapse.

Believe it or not, since you will be shown how to live happily without cigarettes, you will actually *want* to stop smoking. You will quit at your own pace and only when you are ready—and you will be thoroughly prepared.

The only way you can fail is if you are willing to let cigarettes kill you; basically, as long as you keep trying, you will never fail.

You may get so excited about quitting that you want to quit ahead of schedule. Don't. Make yourself wait and finish the program. Do every exercise and try every suggestion in order to quit with as little trauma as possible.

Write your primary motivation for quitting on a separate piece of paper or as part of a journal with a page heading called "Quit Sheet." When cravings start to assault your reason, consult it and it will help you.

During the first week of the program, try to read the first seven chapters in this book. A checklist follows each chapter. Do not continue with the program until you complete every item on the checklist. Try to review the checklists at least once a week to make sure you aren't forgetting anything.

Do not try to quit any other bad habits or addictions at this time, whether they relate to substances or relationships. The only thing you should be focusing on right now is your smoking habit.

When we make an important decision, we often question whether it is correct. This is your mind's way of double checking your decision; it's normal, but don't allow this questioning to go too far. For now, immediately change the subject in your mind.

Living without cigarettes isn't so much a matter of willpower as it is unlearning something you've taught yourself. And what is learned can be unlearned—it may just take a little more time and effort.

So let's start with you.

Understanding Yourself

Do you really want to quit smoking? Can you picture yourself living happily without cigarettes?

If you answered no to the first question, don't waste your time. You are not ready to quit, and chances are you won't. You have to want to quit. You may have to wait until you have the incentive, like an immediate threat to your health.

If you really aren't sure about the second question, this book will help you decide. You need to answer yes to both questions in order to become a permanent nonsmoker with a minimum amount of inner turmoil.

Even if you do answer "yes" to both questions, there is one thing that may stand in your way.

CLINICAL DEPRESSION

Studies have shown that smokers have depression rates three times higher than those of nonsmokers.

Most cases of depression are caused when the brain gradually produces less and less serotonin, the chemical responsible for feelings of well-being, and sleep and appetite regulation. Because this type of depression needs to be treated with medication usually prescribed by a physician, it is called a clinical depression, and medicine, not just positive thinking, is the way to treat it. Clinical depression is not a weakness but a chemical imbalance, like diabetes.

It is estimated that one out of every ten Americans will suffer from depression at some point in their lives. If left untreated, it is likely that it will return for a much longer time and with greater intensity.

The following are symptoms of depression as set forth by the National Institute of Mental Health:

- persistent sad or empty mood
- loss of interest or pleasure in ordinary activities
- loss of interest in sex
- decreased energy, fatigue, getting slowed down
- sleep disturbances (insomnia, early morning waking, or oversleeping)
- eating disturbances (loss of appetite or weight gain)
- difficulty concentrating, remembering, or making decisions
- feelings of guilt, worthlessness, and helplessness
- thoughts of death or suicide, suicide attempts
- irritability
- excessive crying
- chronic aches and pains that don't respond to treatment
- decreased productivity
- safety problems or accidents
- alcohol or drug abuse
- morale problems
- lack of cooperation with others

If you have four or more of these symptoms for more than two weeks, you may be suffering from clinical depression. The good news is that this type of depression has an almost 100 percent cure rate, although it may take four to six weeks for the medication to kick in. There are many different types of medication and new ones are coming out regularly, so if you don't see results within four to six weeks, switch to another.

A natural antidepressant, which accounts for more than 50 percent of the German antidepressant market and is gaining popularity in the United States, is the herb hypericum, also known as St. John's wort. The side effects on record are mild and few, but if you are taking prescription antidepressants or MAO inhibitors or have a preexisting medical or psychiatric condition, consult your doctor before taking St. John's wort.

If you suspect you might be suffering from clinical depression, see a physician before you attempt to quit smoking, since, when you are in a depressed state, smoking may be one of your few pleasures. This can make it very difficult, if not impossible, to quit.

If you are not experiencing four or more of the listed symptoms for more than two weeks, but are often moody, irritable, or unhappy, you may just be a victim of unhealthy thought patterns. You can learn to retrain your mind to stop negative thinking patterns. These are based on habits which can be changed.

YOUR REASONS FOR SMOKING

Below are a list of reasons to continue smoking and rebuttals to them. List your own reasons to smoke if you don't find them here and rebut them if you can.

I'm under too much stress, and cigarettes help me cope.

That's because you have let cigarettes become the way you cope. Most people cope quite well without them, because they have learned how to do so. Coping is a skill you will learn here.

Cigarettes relax me.

On the contrary, cigarettes raise your blood pressure and pump up your heart rate.

Why should I deprive myself of the pleasure?

In the long run, your capacity to experience pleasure will increase, not only because your mental and physical health will improve, but quantitatively as well, since nonsmokers live on the average 18 years longer. Feelings of deprivation will disappear once you've weaned yourself off cigarettes.

I like the taste.

Can you find something a little less deadly to like? Later, you will be shown how to breathe in a manner that will give your lungs almost the same sensation as taking a deep drag of a cigarette.

I can't quit if so-and-so still smokes.

Actually, you can do pretty much anything you want to do; it may just be more difficult.

Cigarettes give my hands something to do, especially in social situations.

What *do* you do with your hands in a social situation where you can't smoke? Once you get the hang of not smoking, it won't bother you anymore, but for now just hang your hands at your sides or stick them in your pockets.

Nobody likes a quitter.

There are usually exceptions to any rule, and this is one of them.

My concentration is better with smoking.

During withdrawal from smoking, your concentration level will probably decrease, but eventually the oxygen content in your blood will increase, and your powers of concentration will be improved.

I can't handle the withdrawal symptoms.

These symptoms will eventually go away. If half of all Americans who ever smoked can quit by successfully ignoring withdrawal symptoms, so can you.

It wouldn't be legal if it were so dangerous.

That's what they said about Pintos.

I'm young, I don't have to worry about that yet.

Many of the diseases caused by cigarettes don't hit old people exclusively. Premature wrinkling and impotence can show up as soon as the early twenties.

I don't smoke enough to worry about it anyway.

Lung cancer risk increases even if you smoke fewer than ten cigarettes a day. No one can predict when a cell is going to become malignant.

I know a woman who smoked for thirty years and she's healthy.

She's lucky.

It's too late—I've done too much damage.

The body begins repairing itself immediately upon quitting. In two weeks your sense of taste and smell return to normal, and your lungs will be working 30 percent better. The risk of heart attack and most cancers decreases substantially after one or more years, except for lung cancer, where the risk is cut in half after ten years. A precancerous cell from the lung of a smoker who stops smoking will just disappear!

Smoking keeps my weight down.

In a recent study of female ex-smokers, most gained only three to six pounds after they quit.

If you are honest with yourself, you will find that most of your reasons can be rebutted, because if cigarettes were necessary to your existence, either physiologically or psychologically, humans would be born dependent upon tobacco. You need to determine whether the advantages of quitting outweigh the disadvantages. If they don't, you might need to wait until the pleasure ratio shifts, but ask yourself first:

- Are the advantages of smoking worth dying a possibly premature or painful death?
- Since you know the withdrawal symptoms and other discomfort will be temporary, is it still worth it to continue smoking?

YOUR REWARDS FOR QUITTING

Some of the rewards are listed below. Choose those from each list that provide you with the greatest motivation and write them on your Quit Sheet. Add your own reasons if you don't find them on this list.

Aging and Cosmetic Rewards

- You will stop promoting the medical syndrome termed "smoker's face," which is characterized by sagging skin, drooping and gaunt facial features, and deep lines around the corners of the mouth and eyes. In one study, 46 percent of long-term smokers were found to have it. Quitting may reverse this to an extent, providing it's not too late.
- You will stop accelerating wrinkle growth.
- You will have a better, glowing, complexion.
- You will look younger.
- You will feel younger.
- You will have a more youthful-sounding voice, one without that raspy telltale smoker's sound.
- You will have cleaner teeth.
- You will deposit less fat around your belly.

Financial Rewards

- You will make more money. A one-pack-a-day smoker will spend approximately $1,000 a year on cigarettes.
- You will save money on health care, as well as on insurance.
- You will save money by not having to replace clothing.
- You will have more job opportunities. More businesses are hiring and promoting nonsmokers, since the average smoker costs the company more in health benefits and sick time.

Health Benefits

- You will reduce your risk of death.
- You will have a longer life expectancy, since 40 percent of smokers die before they reach retirement.
- You will be less vulnerable to diseases such as:
  - lung cancer (risk increases 90 percent)
  - larynx, oral, and throat cancer
  - heart attack (risk can be twice as high)
  - stroke
  - emphysema (where each breath can be a struggle)
  - high blood pressure
  - deteriorating vision or cataracts
  - age-related macular degeneration, the leading cause of blindness among the elderly
- You will breathe more easily and cough less.

And for men:

- You will have less risk of becoming impotent.

And women:

- You will not have as much trouble conceiving a baby.
- You will decrease your risk for miscarrying.
- Your breast milk will no longer be toxic.
- Your risk of giving birth to a mentally retarded child is decreased.
- Your baby's risk of Sudden Infant Death Syndrome (SIDS) is decreased.
- Your risk for breast and cervical cancers is decreased.
- Your menopause may come later.
- Your risk of osteoporosis is decreased.

Mental Rewards

- You will be free from fear of developing tobacco-induced diseases.
- You will have more control over your life.
- You will have more confidence and mental strength.
- You will have more self-respect and will like yourself better.
- You will have a permanent feeling of accomplishment.
- You can finally move forward with your life.
- You will feel better about yourself and have a general sense of well-being, and can face the future squarely.
- You will know yourself better, since your relationship with cigarettes has kept you from being in touch with yourself.
- You will have more energy, and that drained feeling will disappear.
- You will awaken more refreshed and have more motivation.

- Many smokers say they feel they can do anything now that they have quit smoking.

Social Rewards

- You will less likely be viewed as immature or emotionally weak with no self-control.
- Your children will have less chance of taking up the habit.
- Your child's chances of getting chronic infections such as bronchitis and pneumonia are decreased.
- You will no longer have to worry about offending others with the stench of your smoke or stale cigarette smoke on your clothes and in your breath.
- You will get along better with other people, because your relationship with cigarettes may have inhibited your relationships with people.

Everything I've listed is documented (see the References for more information).

---

checklist

✓ If you think you might be suffering from clinical depression, get it treated before beginning this program. Continue with this program only when you have found a treatment that works for you.

✓ List your reasons for continuing to smoke and then counter each one.

✓ Choose one or two rewards you will get by quitting smoking from each of the following categories: cosmetic, financial, health, mental, and social. List them on your Quit Sheet.

Setting Dates

In this chapter, you will be setting two dates—a Quit Day, when you will quit cigarettes for good, and a Rehearsal Day, when you will rehearse being a nonsmoker for twenty-four hours. Setting a date to quit will give you time to prepare.

SETTING YOUR QUIT DAY

On which day of the week would it be easiest for you to refrain from smoking? Which day would be most difficult?

Set your Quit Day so it falls on the day of the week when it would be easiest for you to quit smoking and when you can get in as many days as possible without cigarettes before you hit the most difficult day. If you have a nine-to-five job and suffer from the Monday Blues, you might want to set your Quit Day for Tuesday. That way you would have a couple of nonsmoking days under your belt to prepare for the weekend. However, if more of your triggers to smoke are during the week, you might want to quit on the weekend.

The Quit Day should also be a day when you don't have major projects due at work or school—when you don't expect anything stressful to happen. If possible, schedule quitting around a time when your surroundings and/or routine are completely different—during vacations or holidays, for example, as long as they don't involve strong triggers such as partying.

Make your Quit Day within six to eight weeks from today's date. If you make it earlier, you won't be prepared; if you make it later, you may lose your resolve or forget the techniques.

Once you set a date for your Quit Day, write it on your Quit Sheet and your calendar. Tell your family and friends. You won't be so tempted to procrastinate, because you'll have something tangible at stake, your credibility.

SETTING YOUR REHEARSAL DAY

The Rehearsal Day should be scheduled approximately one week before your Quit Day, on the day of the week it would be *most* difficult for you to quit. Write the date for your rehearsal on your Quit Sheet and mark it on your calendar.

FOR WOMEN

If you suffer from premenstrual syndrome (PMS), you may want to schedule your Quit Day not during or directly before your menses. Smoking makes PMS worse. Try to eat foods which contain more magnesium and B_6. Try to avoid foods high in calcium.

checklist

✓ Figure out which day of the week would be the easiest for you to quit and which day would be the most difficult.

✓ Set your Quit Day six to eight weeks from today, on one of the days it would be easiest for you to quit, as far away as possible before your most difficult day.

✓ Write your Quit Day on your Quit Sheet and your calendar. Tell your family and friends about it.

✓ Set your Rehearsal Day approximately one week before your Quit Day, on the day of the week it would be most difficult for you not to smoke.

✓ Write your Rehearsal Day on your Quit Sheet and on your calendar. Tell your family and friends about it.

Practicing Quitting

You will now have six to eight weeks of training to quit smoking. By the time Quit Day arrives, you will be ready.

PRACTICE WITHHOLDING

What are your favorite foods, drinks, and activities? List all of them on a separate sheet of paper in your journal under the heading "Favorites Sheet."

These are things you will not indulge in or do until Quit Day. Coffee or alcohol shouldn't be on this list since both are related to smoking.

You might have mixed feelings about this, but it is absolutely essential to the program and will be very helpful to you for three reasons:

- You will have some degree of compensation when you quit cigarettes altogether.
- You will have something to look forward to when you quit.
- It is good practice to discipline yourself, and it will give you the practice you are going to need for something tougher—cigarettes.

Smoke a cigarette instead of consuming your favorite food or drink. Try not to break down, even if this food or drink is right in front of you and you have a strong craving for it.

Stop your favorite activities as well, as long as they are not vital to your emotional or physical well-being. Basically, anything you do for the sheer pleasure of doing it should be listed on the Favorites Sheet.

FILLING THE VOID WITH SUBSTITUTES

You are going to learn to use substitutes to help fill the void when you stop smoking. Initially you might not find anything as satisfying as smoking, but once your addiction fades, and it will in time, not smoking will become far more rewarding.

If one substitute doesn't work, try another, but once you choose a substitute, give it more than one chance to work.

YOUR SMOKING STYLE

Next time you light up a cigarette, ask yourself, "Why am I smoking this particular cigarette? Does it help me cope? Relax me? Stimulate me? Give me something to fiddle with? Satisfy a craving? Or is it just a mindless gesture?"

Like most smokers, cigarettes probably serve many different purposes. This program will teach you how to allow other things to fulfill these purposes. You can do this with a minimum amount of stress, if you do it slowly and properly.

Crutch Cigarettes

Crutch Cigarettes are used to cope with nervousness, frustration, anger, etc., and to help you feel better. Use these substitutes:

- Distract yourself.
- Work on a goal.

- Reroute your thoughts.
- Notice life.
- Replace each negative thought with five positive ones.
- Go to a movie.
- Garden or water the plants.
- Walk around the block.
- Drink a glass of water.
- Do a chore.
- Call a friend.
- Read.
- File your fingernails.
- Exercise.
- Use a relaxation technique.
- Count to ten.

Relaxation Cigarettes

Relaxation Cigarettes are used for pure pleasure. They seem to help you relax or provide you with moments of peace during a hectic day. Use these substitutes:

- Work on your goal.
- Use a relaxation technique.
- Take deep breaths.
- Read.
- Give and receive hugs.
- Eat low-fat snacks.
- Take a bath.
- Garden or water the plants.
- Walk around the block.

- Drink a glass of water.
- Call a friend.
- Paint.
- File your fingernails.
- Write a letter.
- Count to ten.
- Go to a movie.
- Go shopping.
- Sleep.
- Reroute your thoughts.

Stimulation Cigarettes

Stimulation Cigarettes are used to help motivate you. Use these substitutes:

- Take deep breaths.
- Use a relaxation technique.
- Give and receive hugs.
- Walk around the block.
- Swallow a dab of toothpaste.
- Wash your face.
- Take a bath.
- Exercise.
- Reroute your thoughts.
- Work on a goal.
- Do a chore.

Handling Cigarettes

Handling Cigarettes are used as an outlet for nervousness. Use these substitutes:

- Squeeze a tennis ball.
- Drink a glass of water.
- Take deep breaths.
- Garden or water the plants.
- Walk around the block.
- Floss.
- Chew on a straw or a toothpick.
- Brush your teeth.
- Play with a Slinky.
- Squeeze a toy.
- Eat a snack.
- Doodle.
- Give and receive hugs.
- Use a relaxation technique.
- File your fingernails.
- Exercise.
- Snap a rubber band on your wrist.
- Work on a goal.
- Do a chore.

Craving Cigarettes

Craving Cigarettes are the physical part of the addiction, but they can also be created by your mind. Use these substitutes:

- Take deep breaths.
- Use nicotine gum, patch, or nasal spray.
- Take Zyban.
- Use clove oil.
- Drink a glass of water.

- Distract yourself.
- Do a chore.
- Use a relaxation technique.
- Read.
- Swallow a dab of toothpaste.
- Drink a glass of water.
- Exercise.

Mindless Cigarettes

Mindless Cigarettes are those lit or smoked without conscious thought. Use these substitutes:

- Make your cigarettes difficult to find.
- Take deep breaths.
- Change your routine.
- Smoke with the opposite hand than the one you usually use.
- Snap a rubber band around your wrist.

PRACTICE SESSIONS

Between now and your Quit Day, your goal will be to try to replace every type of cigarette you smoke with a substitute that most closely matches the purpose that particular cigarette is serving for you.

Try to practice at least four times a day. For each practice session, substitute one type of cigarette.

If you have decided to give in to a craving for a particular cigarette, allow yourself to smoke, but wait at least ten more minutes and then note exactly how long you resisted the craving. The next time you run into that same situation, whether that day or another day, refrain for a longer time than the last time by at least ten minutes. Do not allow yourself to smoke in that triggering situation again without first trying to substitute for it.

Once you have substituted for every type of cigarette three times or more, just start over. The focus here should be on concentrating on what the biggest causes for relapse are, like drinking alcohol or coffee, as well as negative emotions. The more practice you do, the easier it will be for you to quit cigarettes altogether.

Try to plan the night before which cigarettes you will substitute for and which substitute(s) you will use. If you didn't plan your practice session the night before, try to plan in advance as much as you can. When planning your practice session, always visualize yourself saying "No thanks," and then successfully using the substitute(s). The proper visualization technique will be outlined later (see page 51).

Quit the easy situations and emotions first. Make a telephone call and don't smoke. Don't smoke when something annoys you. Progress to having a cup of coffee without smoking or not smoking when you are irritated. Finally, visit your friends who smoke without smoking.

Whenever you find your resolve weakening during a practice session, do thought-stopping exercises. Thought-stopping is accomplished by saying to yourself (or out loud if you can get away with it), "Stop!" and then changing the subject in your mind. Another way to change the subject is to concentrate solely on what one or more of your senses is experiencing right then. It isn't necessary to package your perceptions with words, just observe.

Tell yourself you can have a cigarette in five minutes if you absolutely have to. Usually, you will find that more than five minutes have passed before you need to remind yourself that you wanted to smoke that cigarette. You may wonder how much you really needed to smoke that cigarette if it wasn't important enough to keep in your head for five minutes. If cravings are something you absolutely can't ignore, why do you forget about them?

If it is getting close to Rehearsal Day and you can't seem to quit in a particular situation—for example, not smoking while visiting your smoker friends, or not smoking when you are angry—just keep trying and go longer than the last time by ten minutes.

Expect setbacks. Never condemn yourself for not reaching your goal of abstaining from smoking for a triggering situation or emotion.

Just don't stop trying. This way you will at least have some practice dealing with those difficult triggers. You will also know to avoid these situations for as long as you possibly can once your Quit Day arrives.

Notice which triggering situations are most difficult for you, so you can prepare for Quit Day and beyond. Write these under a heading called "Main Triggers" on the Quit Sheet.

If you are not in the mood to try a substitute, do it anyway.

Building a sense of accomplishment with successful practice sessions will build your confidence and show you that you *can* cope, and cope well, without cigarettes. The more you practice, the easier it gets.

NOTES ON DIFFERENT SUBSTITUTES

Since a cigarette often serves more than one purpose, you will often need to use more than one substitute at a time.

For example, cravings will accompany many, if not most, of your cigarette triggers, so if you feel the need for a Crutch Cigarette as well as a physical Craving Cigarette, chew some nicotine gum to deal with the craving part and then stretch to alleviate some tension while you try to reroute your thoughts. Use as many substitutes as you have at your disposal.

If one of your substitutes worked for a trigger once but didn't work another time, the cigarette probably served another purpose as well, so combine substitutes from the applicable lists.

Deep Breathing

Deep breathing nearly duplicates the full feeling in your lungs as a deep drag on a cigarette, but that's where the similarity ends. Accompany all of your substitutes with a few deep breaths. Once you condition yourself to take deep breaths with each craving, you will find yourself doing this unconsciously, for example, while you're watching someone on TV smoking. It's also a great way to calm yourself.

Nicotine Gum, Patch, or Nasal Spray

If you smoke many cigarettes in response to physical cravings, you will find nicotine replacement therapy very helpful.

It is a good idea to get a doctor's advice before using nicotine replacement therapy. Although rare, heart attacks have been reported in people who smoked while wearing the patch, and the gum and nasal spray may also have some side effects. If you have had certain illnesses, you may be advised against nicotine replacement therapy. For the nasal spray, a doctor's prescription is necessary. If you need to see a doctor, do it before Quit Day.

Do not use the gum, patch, or nasal spray until your Quit Day, because you could get an overdose of nicotine if you continue to smoke. Once you have gone through Quit Day and are no longer smoking, nicotine gum is a good replacement for physical cravings.

Zyban and Clonidine

Zyban is the first nicotine-free stop-smoking drug to be available in the United States. As with any other drug, it has possible side effects, so a doctor's prescription is necessary. Although it's expensive, studies show quitting rates rise to 58 percent when Zyban is combined with the patch.

Clonidine is another drug that some people use to alleviate withdrawal symptoms due to quitting. You will also need a doctor's prescription for it.

Water

Water not only cleans out your lungs (it removes mucus), but your entire system. Since most of us don't drink the recommended six to eight glasses per day, this would be a good time to get into the habit of drinking water.

Snacks

When using snacks as a substitute, remember that favorite foods are not included in your choice of snacks. Consider only low-fat and low- or no-sugar snacks.

Sugar acts like nicotine, in that the more you eat or smoke, the more you want. Too much sugar also puts you at risk for the Sugar Blues, the last thing you need when you quit. You may crave sweets or salt after you quit smoking, so be careful how you snack.

Other than that, don't worry about what kind of other bad habits you might be cultivating by using snacks as a substitute. Right now, the most important thing is to break the cigarette habit, since this is one of the hardest habits to break. Heroin may be easier to kick than nicotine.

Try picking some snacks from the following list: apples, artichokes, beef jerky, berries, bread sticks, carrots, celery, Cheez-its, cinnamon or flavored toothpicks, cinnamon sticks, crackers, cup of decaf tea, dried fruit, fresh fruit, gum, grapes, hard candy, honey, licorice, lollipops, mints, nuts in the shell, peaches, pears, pickles, pomegranates, popcorn, potato chips, pretzels, pumpkin seeds, radishes, raisins, oranges, sorbet, sugarless gum, sunflower seeds, tangerines, vegetables, watermelon.

NOTE: Sunflower seeds are rumored to quell nicotine craving. Although this has never been scientifically proven, they seem to work for some people. Try the shelled type, to give your mouth a little something extra to do.

Toothpaste

Toothpaste might also be an effective aid against cigarette smoking. Brush your teeth with a lot of toothpaste. Now inhale a cigarette. How does it taste? Some people find the cigarette tastes repugnant after the toothpaste, while others don't notice a difference. How about you?

Clove Oil

Clove oil also seems to take away the urge to smoke for some people. Put a drop on your finger and apply it to the back of your tongue. If it works, you can find it at most health food stores.

Flavored Antacid Tablets

Studies have shown that anxiety and stress may cause high acid content in urine. Since there have also been studies which link acidity in the stomach to a propensity to smoke, try a Tums™ or other flavored antacid tablet.

Relaxation Techniques, Exercise, and Goals

These substitutes, which will improve your lifestyle, will be covered in detail in the next chapter.

Chores

No one's life is free from responsibilities, which often translate into chores. If we try to ignore them, we only cause more trouble and stress.

So instead of using one time period to accomplish one unappealing task, use the same time period to accomplish two or more tasks that you have been postponing. For example, while you are defying a craving, why not dust or read an article or part of one you have been wanting to read. Tax returns would fit nicely into this plan. Start by sorting just enough receipts to fill the length of time it takes to smoke a cigarette.

The idea is to make something pleasant that isn't pleasant to contemplate and to decrease the time you have to spend doing chores by completing two or more of them within the same period. This will give you more time for fun. Chores are good substitutes for Craving, Handling, Stimulation, and Crutch Cigarettes.

When your Quit Day arrives, you may not feel like doing much of anything (besides maybe sulking), let alone chores. Don't use chores as a substitute at first when you quit. Wait until you feel more comfortable about not smoking, unless the chore is something that absolutely cannot wait.

PRACTICE RESISTING TRIGGERS

At least two of your practice sessions each day should be devoted to resisting two of the most powerful triggers—your emotions and your need to relax.

Experience every emotion or combination of emotions, whether pleasant or unpleasant, in as many different situations as possible without smoking between now and Rehearsal Day. This should be done at least three times for each situation, preferably more. Make handling emotions your priority.

Of course, feelings don't usually appear or disappear on command. If you run into an unusual emotion or feeling, take the opportunity to turn it into an impromptu practice session, and try to work through it without smoking. Light up only when the feeling has safely subsided.

Relaxation Cigarettes are related to cigarettes triggered by emotions. Make sure another one of your practice sessions each day consists of substituting a Relaxation Cigarette with a relaxation technique effective for you. This will be explored in more detail in the "Exchanging Your Lifestyle" chapter.

SMOKING UNTIL REHEARSAL DAY

Between now and Rehearsal Day, except for your practice sessions, you are free to smoke to your heart's content. And for Rehearsal Day, make sure you have some full ashtrays.

After Rehearsal Day you won't have to do any more practice sessions unless you haven't completed three practice sessions for a certain trigger or you have the opportunity to practice on a triggering situation or emotion that hasn't come up before.

Do not taper off or cut down on your smoking. Besides being the most agonizing way to quit, this method has a recidivism rate three times higher than going cold turkey, probably in large part because it generates feelings of deprivation.

Do not change to cigarettes with less tar and nicotine and do not use filters. You are not supposed to feel deprived of cigarettes in any way. Smokers tend to drag more deeply on lighter cigarettes anyway.

Do not use cigars or a pipe as a substitute for cigarettes. Don't use any substitute that is physically addicting, like sugar, smokeless tobacco, or drugs.

Although you may smoke as many cigarettes as you like, do cut out all Mindless Cigarettes—cigarettes you light without thinking—smoke only those you really want or think you need.

While you are smoking, eat in a healthy way, exercise, and get plenty of sleep.

Vitamin A is the most important nutrient for healthy tissues lining the bronchi, trachea, and lungs. Try eating carrots, broccoli, asparagus, apricots, and cantaloupes for this vitamin.

Antioxidants such as vitamins C and E can block the formation of cancer-causing substances. You can find these vitamins in citrus fruits, green peppers, cantaloupes, and broccoli. To boost your immune system, take extra vitamin C, which smoking depletes your system of.

Selenium helps to detoxify heavy metals such as mercury and cadmium in cigarette smoke. The National Cancer Institute recommends 50–200 mcg of selenium per day.

A recent study reports that men who smoked more than a pack a day and exercised regularly had a 30 percent lower death rate due to cancer or heart disease. Exercise is discussed further in the next chapter. Also reduce your cancer risk by eating more fruits, vegetables, and whole grains, and fewer smoked, pickled, or cured foods. Drink alcohol in moderation. Avoid food additives and animal fat (meats, butter, and cheese), and moderate your intake of monounsaturated fats (olive oil) and unsaturated fats (corn and safflower oil).

checklist

- ✓ List all of your favorite foods, drinks, and activities on the Favorites Sheet.

- ✓ Ignore everything on the Favorites Sheet until Quit Day, unless it is specifically related to smoking, like coffee or alcohol.

- ✓ Find out what purpose you let each cigarette serve for you. Does it help you cope, relax or stimulate you, satisfy a craving, give you something to play with, or is it just a mindless gesture?

- ✓ Plan at least four practice sessions for each day, if possible. Choose which substitute(s) you will be using from the appropriate list for that cigarette, and visualize using that substance.

- ✓ Try to find a substitute for each type of cigarette you usually smoke in response to every triggering situation, at least three times by the time you reach Quit Day.

- ✓ Whenever you find your resolve weakening during a practice session, do thought-stopping exercises.

- ✓ If you don't succeed in a practice session for a particular cigarette, try again the very next time that triggering situation comes up. Do not allow yourself to smoke in that triggering situation again without first trying to find a substitute for it.

(continued)

✓ Don't condemn yourself for setbacks.

✓ Notice what is the trigger for most of your cigarettes. Write this down on the Quit Sheet.

✓ Accompany all of your substitutes with a few deep breaths.

✓ Use nicotine gum, the patch, or nasal spray if you find that many of your cigarettes are smoked in response to physical cravings.

✓ Ask your doctor about getting a prescription for Zyban.

✓ Try toothpaste, flavored antacid tablets, clove oil, and sunflower seeds to see if they alleviate your cravings for cigarettes.

✓ Try to get into the habit of accomplishing at least two unpleasant tasks within the same time period.

✓ Make sure at least two of your practice sessions each day are devoted to resisting two of your most powerful triggers—your feelings and your need to relax.

✓ Once you start duplicating practice sessions, make handling emotions your priority.

✓ Other than your practice sessions and Rehearsal Day, smoke your regular brand as much or as little as usual, but do cut out Mindless Cigarettes.

✓ Live as healthfully as possible while you are smoking and do what you can to combat the harmful effects of smoking.

Exchanging Your Lifestyle

This chapter focuses on the substitutes that will ease you out of your cigarette-oriented lifestyle and into a more mentally and physically healthier, and thereby happier, one.

RELAXING

Smokers often forget how to cope with stress and tension because they have allowed cigarettes to do that job for them. But since cigarettes raise your blood pressure and speed your heart rate, you will be more relaxed if you don't smoke.

Relaxing takes practice, but don't give up. Keep trying to go a little further each time, by taking a few more breaths or relaxing a little more. You may not always have successful relaxation sessions, but if you keep trying, you will become a more relaxed person.

Noticing Life

Do you ever ask yourself where all the years have gone? Do you ever feel that you are missing out on something, although you are not quite sure what? Do you feel you are often just going through the motions without truly experiencing things? Do you feel as if you are not quite in touch with life? Do some people seem to enjoy life more than you? Watch yourself. Notice how often you are doing it but not fully enjoying or experiencing it.

If you don't pay attention to and consciously experience life, it will pass you by. The more you notice life, the fuller it becomes.

Because we use cigarettes to filter our feelings and experiences, learning to live without them, by removing the filter, will lead to a richer and more fulfilled life.

The key to making your life fuller is simple: Focus in on your surroundings by paying as much attention as you can to what each of your five senses are experiencing. The more you become aware of what your senses are experiencing, the more you will experience moments of inexplicable joy.

Schedule six days a week to learn to better appreciate your senses. For example, designate the seeing sense for Mondays, hearing for Tuesdays, smelling for Wednesdays, tasting for Thursdays, and touching for Fridays. The sixth day is the day to take some time to pay attention to what all of your senses are experiencing. If you have trouble getting solid impressions from all senses, work on your strongest sense first, and go from there.

Pay attention throughout the day. How many different sounds can you hear? Try to notice something you have never noticed before. Don't do anything else, if possible; just concentrate on observing as much as you can in as much detail as possible. You may not be able to keep this up for more than a few seconds, but pay attention for as long as possible. When you have cravings, take some deep breaths and fully concentrate on your target sense.

Don't worry if you forget to pay attention or if the reality is too painful to focus on. Just get into the habit of becoming more aware of your surroundings in general. This will bring meaning to the little everyday activities of your life as well as the more dramatic moments.

Deep Breathing

Breathing deeply immediately relaxes you by promoting the flow of oxygen to your brain and throughout your entire body. Oxygen also produces energy and is good for your overall health.

To breathe properly, sit in a comfortable position, close your eyes, and relax your muscles. Inhale to a count of eight (1-1000, 2-1000, etc.), pause for a count of one, then exhale to a count of six, pause for a count of one, and repeat until you feel even a little bit more relaxed. When inhaling your abdomen rises first, then the bottom half of your lungs, then the top half. It is not necessary to cram your lungs with air—keep it comfortable.

Release physical and mental tension with each breath. Let go of any thoughts that come to your mind and tell yourself you will consider them later. Replace thoughts of the past or the future with thoughts only of what is happening right now.

Practice breathing more deeply any time you can. Remember to accompany all of your substitutes with a few deep breaths and use them to otherwise thwart cigarette cravings.

Meditation

There are as many ways of meditating as there are religions—Western as well as Eastern.

There are four types of brain waves—beta, alpha, theta, and delta. Beta waves generate the most cycles (13–30 Hz, or up to 100 Hz when excited). The next slowest are alpha waves, which are associated with calmness and relaxation. Theta waves appear before falling asleep or awakening (4–7 Hz), and delta waves appear when you are in a deep sleep.

Meditation increases the presence of alpha brain waves, which are associated with calmness and relaxation. Regular meditation has a number of benefits: better concentration, decreased anxiety and depression, enhanced senses, enhanced spiritual awareness, happy feelings, greater peace of mind, higher self-esteem, improved digestion, increased efficiency, increased creativity, more frequent peak moments, more pleasant emotions, protection for the heart, protection against high blood pressure, quicker onset and better quality of sleep.

Meditation will not always calm you, but it will help you to become a less stressful person. Meditating for fifteen minutes in the morning and fifteen minutes at night will help you to center yourself, but you can also meditate for as short a time as one minute or for as long a time as it would have taken to smoke a cigarette.

Begin all meditations with deep breaths, releasing tension from your body with each breath. Try the following techniques and choose one or more for you.

Relaxing from Head to Toe

Relax every muscle in your body inch by inch, starting with your head. Allow ten to thirty seconds for each part of your body to relax more and more. Once you are relaxed, imagine a waterfall washing away the stress throughout your body, starting with your head. See the tension being released through your toes.

Vary this exercise by contracting the muscles in your toes as hard as you can, then releasing, letting all tension flow out. Then tense up your feet and release, your ankles, and so on, until you reach the top of your head.

You can also visualize an image for tension and then replace it with an image for relaxation. For example, if your stomach is tense, imagine that tension red or picture the tension in a cable or give it the sound of a jackhammer or the smell of a dentist's office.

Let the tension fade to pastel blue, the cable slacken, the jackhammer lessen, the dentist's office smell like a rose. See yourself days or years from now when the pain has long passed. Tell yourself that you will survive it.

Focusing on Now

When you live in the present moment, all your attention is focused only on what you are doing right now. There is no room for anything else to enter—fears, desires, any stressors.

You do not have to place yourself in seclusion or sit silently in order to meditate. The goal of meditation is to focus all your attention on the present moment, the inhale, the exhale, the mantra or—the food!

For this tasty meditation, get your favorite food and sit in a comfortable spot. Take a few deep breaths and notice the color, size, shape, and texture of the food. Is it appealing to you? Notice every part of eating, starting with reaching toward the food, lifting it up, and then bringing it to your mouth. Try to pick out the different smells. Then feel your teeth penetrate the food. Where is your tongue while all of this is happening? What is it tasting? And where is your arm? How far down the esophagus can you track the food? Try to be aware of as many sensations as you can.

You can do this exercise for any of your regular routines—brushing your teeth or hair, washing dishes, raking leaves, anything. Just be sure not to rush.

Massage

Massage is a good way to release the tension that gets stored in muscles, as well as to promote relaxation. If you can't afford a massage, buy a little hand-held massager and have your significant other massage you with it, especially when you want to overcome a craving.

Aromatherapy

Aromatherapy has been used for emotional and physical healing as far back as 4000 B.C.E.

The cilia in your nostrils are located on top of about ten million olfactory receptors located in your nose. The cilia detect odors. This information is transported to the limbic region, which is responsible for producing hormones that affect appetite, body temperature, insulin production, metabolism, stress levels, and sex drive. The limbic region also affects the nervous system, including moods, desires, motivation, intuition, and creativity, by stimulating the release of neurotransmitters and endorphins in your brain.

Aromatherapy helps to bring about a more balanced state by aiding relaxation. Try the pleasant smells from the past or present that have the capacity to relax you—lotions, perfumes, incense, or scented oils.

In *Pocket Guide to Aromatherapy*, herbalist Kathi Keville recommends the following essential oils to help reduce stress: basil, bergamot, cardamom, clove, chamomile, clary sage, frankincense, helicrysum, jasmine, lavender, marjoram, melissa, myrrh, neroli, nutmeg, orange, pettigrain, rose, sandalwood, valerian, vanilla, and ylang-ylang.

Music

Baroque music is relaxing to most people. At one beat per second, it follows the natural rhythm of the heart and breathing. Listen to Bach, Handel, and Telemann.

The electric piano, flute, and harp can relax you, as do sounds that echo. Also try songs you liked from your childhood.

Pet Your Pet

It is well known that interacting with your pet can have a therapeutic effect for the both of you. Studies have shown that pets can also suffer from depression if they do not get enough attention. The next time you need to relax and think of lighting up, try petting your pet.

Humor

It is difficult to stay anxious, angry, or depressed when you are laughing. Humor helps us solve problems and also connects us to people. Close your eyes and relax, and picture using humor in a difficult situation. Try to see the funny side of everything. Laugh at yourself with acceptance, not with derision. If this isn't easy for you, pretend until you get the hang of it.

Read a funny book or watch a comedy on TV. Start a humor library with clippings of cartoons, jokes, or funny stories—anything that makes you smile. During Quit Day and afterward, you can pull out this file.

Laughter puts things into perspective, and gives you emotional control. Try to grab every opportunity to use humor to smooth your way through life.

Playing

The more evolved an animal is, the more likely the animal will play. So, if humans are the most evolved animals, our need for play will be even greater. Playing makes our lives more meaningful and increases our energy.

Play is anything you engage in just for fun. It serves as a diversion from work and our everyday problems. It is not related to work, and it doesn't necessarily involve competition.

Play could be a hobby that has always attracted you, or just a simple way to have more fun. Listen to music while lying on your stomach on the floor. Play a musical instrument, read a poem, do a jigsaw or crossword puzzle, or snuggle with your partner. Try to do something fun every day, so you can fill your past with good memories.

EXERCISING

There is an old Asian saying, "Those who don't find time for exercise will have to find time for illness."

The benefits of exercise are vast. It helps you relieve stress and prevent insomnia. It's good for every part of your body. People who exercise are statistically less likely (60 percent) to get cancer and osteoporosis. Regular exercise keeps the brain sharp. Memory loss need not be inevitable for old people.

When exercising, follow these guidelines:

- Start off slowly, maybe ten minutes three times a week, and work up from there.
- Get into the habit of exercising regularly, but just do what you can.

- Never criticize yourself if you are slacking off once in a while. Instead, praise yourself for how well you have been doing.

If you have always wanted to have a flat stomach, large biceps, or a firmer derriere, do a few exercises for that part of your body as a substitute for smoking.

Although the couch may be a very comfortable place to hang out, by being inactive you are cheating yourself of a full life. If you engage in a little activity first, and then retreat to the couch, you can have the best of both worlds. Being active is just a habit. To develop any new habit may take some effort, but it will soon become effortless.

Instead of thinking how much you hate to exercise before you go to the gym, skip that part and visualize the end result, like fitting into a smaller size or a great bathing suit.

Cardiovascular Exercise

Cardiovascular exercise strengthens your cardiovascular system and increases your stamina. It also produces endorphins, the brain's natural "upper." Endorphins help you relax and lead to increased mental alertness. Don't expect to experience the benefits of endorphin production much until after withdrawal symptoms disappear, however, since initially, withdrawal symptoms may be too overwhelming for you to notice much else.

Cardiovascular exercise can also count as play time when you are doing something you really like. Try basketball, mountain biking, dancing, rollerblading, or tennis for some fun.

As little as twenty minutes of cardiovascular exercise three times a week can improve your fitness. You can expect to see external results within a couple of months.

Stretching

Stretching relaxes you, increases muscle strength and flexibility, and improves circulation, which keeps you more alert. It can even reverse some of the symptoms of aging. Stretching can be done almost any-where—at your desk at work, in the car, or while you watch TV.

Any muscle can be stretched. Choose a muscle or group of mus-cles and stretch for thirty seconds, relax and repeat. Gradually work up to stretching for two minutes at a time. Add in some deep breaths and you will see how relaxing this can be.

There are many good books on stretching, if you want to follow a more structured approach. Yoga may also be useful.

Muscle Toning

Toning exercises focus on firming or toning muscles. There are two basic ways to tone muscles.

Isometrics use resistance without movement. For example, by pushing your hands together, you can tone your arms and upper chest. You can tone your thigh by tightening the thigh muscle.

Isotonics use resistance through movement to contract muscles. Push-ups for the arms and chests or squats for the thighs and buttocks are examples. To tone muscles, use frequent repetitions and less resis-tance. To build up muscles, use less repetitions and more resistance.

GOALS

This substitute involves taking steps toward a goal that will improve your life. It could be a goal that you haven't had the time to work on, something you planned to do when you quit smoking, or some-thing you put off because you didn't find the effort particularly appealing.

You will be shown how to choose a goal. Once you have done this, the steps needed to achieve that goal will serve as your substi-tutes.

Helping Yourself

What would make you happier? Have you always wanted to play a musical instrument, learn more about the Internet, or maybe even make a major change in your life? When choosing a personal goal, choose something that you believe will make your life a little or a lot happier.

Helping Others or the Environment

Charity work can boost your self-esteem, as well as make you feel less lonely. There are many types of volunteer work that can be done in your home within the time it takes to smoke one cigarette.

- Make a telephone call.
- Fold flyers.
- Address envelopes.
- Compose a paragraph of a newsletter.
- Look up your congressperson's name and address.
- Answer a crisis hotline telephone call to your home.
- Create an idea for a community service.
- Clean out part of your closet for charity.
- Send a fax or e-mail to help with a cause. (Many organizations on the Internet will tell you how your e-mail can help in their latest campaign.)

Don't feel like you have to help; do it only if it is something you really want to do. It is only from this approach that you will experience "helper's high." If you don't feel like physically doing anything, you could also put some, or all, of the money you would have otherwise spent on a pack of cigarettes into a fund for your favorite charity.

Preparing a Goal to Work as a Substitute

Make a list of things you have always wanted to do for yourself and for others, yet didn't have the time or motivation. If you had only twenty-four hours to live, would you be satisfied with the way you have lived your life so far?

On a separate sheet of paper or in your journal, make a page titled "Goals Sheet." Write down your goal(s), and then write down each step toward accomplishing your goal, breaking the steps down so that you can accomplish each step within the time it takes to combat a cigarette craving. The steps can be as small as calling the library to reserve a book on choosing a new career, to browsing through a book on volunteerism to see if there are any causes that arouse your passion.

Every time you work on your goal, picture how reaching it will make you happier. By using a step or even part of a step as a substitute, you will come closer and closer to reaching your goal. Devote as little or as much time to each step as you like, until the craving disappears or at least becomes manageable.

checklist

✓ Choose a relaxation technique and practice it every day, if only for a few minutes.

✓ Learn to breathe properly and use deep breathing with all your substitutes, as well as any time you feel tense.

✓ Consider an exercise program to use as a substitute.

✓ Choose a personal goal for yourself, and perhaps another goal to help others or the environment.

✓ Break the goal(s) down into as many small steps as possible, and use each step or part of a step as a substitute.

Building Your Smokefree Reality

You will need to fortify your new smokefree reality, to brace it against withdrawal symptoms, which have the potential to play havoc with your judgment and threaten your conviction to quit.

This chapter will show you how to get a more accurate perspective for those times. You will also learn how to survive withdrawal symptoms relatively easily, to the point where you might even enjoy the challenge.

YOUR PERCEPTIONS

Your mind is the most powerful force shaping you and your life. You choose the way you want to look at and perceive things. You choose the way you perceive things, the way you react to anything, the way you see yourself.

You will learn to harness both the forces of perception and your subconscious to make them work. It takes practice, but everyone has the power to make her/his own reality.

Studies have shown that if you act "as if " you were the person you want to be, you will eventually become that person. Try the simple exercise below.

Spend a brief moment pretending that you are already a non-smoker and that you do not want a cigarette and you do not miss smoking. You may have to lie to yourself most of the time, but say it to yourself anyway, especially whenever a craving hits. Say to yourself these four things, even if you don't believe them:

- I am a nonsmoker now.
- I do not want a cigarette.
- I do not miss cigarettes.
- I am much better off without cigarettes.

The brain is made up of information pathways, which become more established the more you use them. That's why a phone number you regularly dial stays in your head. By rerouting your dependence on cigarettes into more independent thoughts, you start training your thinking patterns into new and different pathways.

Begin to think of living without cigarettes not as a loss but as a reward, since you will be gaining a better life in the long run. See quitting smoking not as losing a friend, but as dumping a treacherous foe.

WITHDRAWAL SYMPTOMS

Addiction induces compulsiveness, not only while you are engaging in the addictive behavior, but also when you begin to stop it. This compulsiveness manifests itself in withdrawal symptoms.

Withdrawal symptoms have the potential to rob you of your good sense. Become acquainted with the following list of withdrawal symptoms.

- aggressiveness
- anger
- anxiety
- chest pains

- concentration problems
- constipation
- coughing
- cravings
- crying
- decreased ability to tolerate stress
- decreased sex drive
- depression
- dreams about smoking
- fatigue
- grouchiness
- headaches
- hunger
- impaired work performance
- increased phlegm
- irritability
- lack of energy
- nervousness
- restlessness
- short temper
- sleep disturbances
- sleepiness
- sore throat
- spaciness
- stomach pains

You may feel as if the only way to end the discomfort is to smoke. But waiting it out won't kill you, it won't even traumatize you. Dizziness and coughing will go away in a few days. The other symptoms may take one to two weeks.

The strongest withdrawal symptoms will come in the form of cravings. Cravings are a natural part of quitting any addiction:

- Deep breaths are the best way to combat them.
- Changing the subject in your mind is the second best way.
- They will last a short time.
- They get shorter, less intense, and farther apart in time, and finally they will become a rarity or disappear.

You may experience cravings shortly after you have told yourself you have smoked your last cigarette. This is your mind testing you. How well you handle these cravings will make all the difference in the world as to how painless and effective quitting will be.

Cravings should always be greeted with a few deep breaths and then escorted right out of your mind, using thought-stopping.

Don't give the voices which you hear under the duress of withdrawal any credibility. A common thought is "I must be making a mistake if I am in so much pain." But why should these feelings be more accurate than the ones you had when you are weren't suffering from separation anxiety—the ones that said, "I really need to quit smoking"?

Habits can be either good or bad. You know a habit is bad for you if:

- It doesn't accomplish anything, but costs you time and energy.
- It draws you away from natural experiences.
- It is physically harmful.
- It irritates people.
- It makes you look foolish.
- You don't approve of it yourself.

Whenever you experience an onset of self-doubt, do your thought-stopping exercises. Of course, for more fun and games, the mind will return to the very topic you don't want to think about, and the more you worry about it, the longer it will go on. Nonchalantly and persistently, continue to change the subject in your mind until another one finally sticks. Just think (with a yawn), "Next..."

VISUALIZING SUCCESS

Visualization is a way of working with your subconscious. By visualizing, you are provided with some measure of practice before the actual attempt. Studies have shown that using visualization helps people to excel in practically everything. Athletes use visualization to help perfect their games.

Visualization is easiest in the morning and at night while lying in bed, although you can do it anywhere. Scan your body and breathe deeply, releasing tension with each exhale. Use music if you wish.

When picturing which cigarettes you will substitute for the next day, always see yourself successfully dealing with the triggering situation by saying "No thanks" (whether the suggestion comes from you or another person), and then using a substitute you have chosen from one of the lists. Visualize the scene again to help cement the image, and add three more things to your visualization:

- feeling happy with your decision
- feeling relieved that you didn't smoke that cigarette
- feeling proud of your strength in handling the situation without smoking

Incorporate as much detail as possible into your visualizations, and involve as many senses as you can. Nudge out any unrelated thoughts.

Now create another visualization. This one will be the new nonsmoking you. The picture should contain your main reasons for wanting to quit smoking. How will you look as a nonsmoker? Will you have a more relaxed attitude? Will you be in better physical shape? Will you be wearing nicer clothes because you have more money?

In your practice sessions, while you are implementing your substitute, incorporate the visualization where you successfully use your substitute, as well as the picture of the new nonsmoking you.

NEUROLINGUISTIC PROGRAMMING (NLP)

Neurolinguistic Programming (NLP) is another way of tapping your subconscious. The following NLP technique of switching dark and light pictures is related to visualization and can be quite effective. Try it in combination with thought-stopping.

Picture Yourself as a Smoker

Take a drag and blow the smoke through a tissue. Notice the yellow residue on the tissue. This is the residue filtered through your lungs. What do you think your lungs look like after puffing hundreds of times a day 365 days a year?

Take a minute to sit back and relax. Picture yourself as smoking away in a darkened room. See your saggy, gray skin wrinkling into telltale lines around your mouth as your blackened lungs painfully hack up mucus. Picture a person standing nearby, someone you admire and respect, whom you may or may not know personally. That person is looking at you with a mixture of revulsion and pity. See your shoulders hunched over with embarrassment. Incorporate any other disadvantages to smoking into your picture.

Picture this scene a few more times to cement it. Use all your senses in visualizing. What do you see, smell, and hear? How do you feel?

Picture Yourself as a Nonsmoker

Picture yourself in a bright, sunny room. See yourself standing tall as you handle your life with assurance. See yourself relieved that you no longer have to worry about cancer or setting a bad example for your kids. That same person from the earlier picture stands nearby and smiles as s/he admires your confidence and poise. Again, use all your senses when visualizing and incorporate any other advantages of quitting into your picture.

Picture this scene a few more times to cement it.

What to Do with These Pictures

It can be disheartening to hear someone say they still crave cigarettes after quitting for so many years. Realize that you will not be able to discard all your good memories of smoking, but you do have the choice to just acknowledge, rather than dwell on, these memories.

Every time you start to reminisce about one of those "good" times, let the dark picture shove that memory aside and then have the bright picture shove the dark picture out of the way.

Do this every time you begin to reminisce about smoking or have a craving, no matter how weak or fleeting the craving might be, and then employ your substitute.

Anchoring Confidence

Another NLP technique called "anchoring" can elicit any type of feeling you want on command. Here we will be using anchoring for the purposes of furnishing you with an extra jolt of confidence whenever you might need it.

Sitting comfortably, close your eyes and take a minute to relax your body. Release tension from the areas that are tight. Rest your hands in your lap and keep them slightly separated.

Now go back in time. Pick a time when you felt good about yourself, when you felt successful or especially confident. If you have trouble finding such a memory, make up a memory; the effect will be the same. When you see that time, take a deep breath and notice everything about it, the sights, sounds, smells, etc. How did you look?

Once you feel the confidence, firmly touch your left wrist with your right hand in a particular spot that you can easily remember. This anchors your feeling of confidence to the touch on your wrist. You will want to be able to duplicate that touch later on.

Recall three or four other memories that give you the same confidence and repeat them, using the same touch in the same spot. The next time you need a confidence boost, touch your wrist in exactly the same way.

THE BUDDY SYSTEM

Although not a requirement, a buddy is strongly recommended and might prove to be invaluable: either a fellow smoker who would like to quit or a nonsmoking family member or friend who would like to see you quit but never nags, judges, or lays guilt trips on you.

Your buddy should be available any time of the day or night to talk to you for Rehearsal Day, Quit Day, and beyond. Ask your buddy to keep track of all the positive things you said about quitting when you successfully used substitutes during practice sessions. Ask her/him to then remind you of how much you wanted to quit when withdrawal symptoms start to rob you of your good sense. These reminders may talk you out of any thoughts you may be entertaining of starting up again.

If your buddy is a fellow smoker, be there for her/him in the same way. Praise your buddy's smallest accomplishments. When setting your Rehearsal Days, set them on different dates, but schedule your Quit Days for the same date.

If your buddy relapses or drops out of the program or asks you to reschedule your Quit Day, don't do it! Just stick with the program and have your buddy read the section on page 91.

CHOOSE A ROLE MODEL

Choose a role model—someone you admire who doesn't smoke, someone who appears confident and self-assured. Watch your role model for the rest of the program. How do they stand? What does their facial expression say about how they feel about themselves? What are their work habits? What do they do with their hands when they are talking to someone? What do they do when they are stressed out? How do they handle it? Ask your role model how they handle stress.

The next time a stressful situation occurs that threatens to weaken your resolve, imagine how your role model would handle the situation and then do the same.

THE JOURNAL

Journals have been widely recognized by mental health professionals as effective aids. This is not to imply that you are mentally ill, but let's face it, how rational is a person who spends healthy sums of money to inhale toxic chemicals? Although keeping a journal might seem a hassle, it will be necessary later in the program.

A journal is a good way to purge yourself of the day's hurts and disappointments. Writing helps to identify the pain and make sense of it. And by acknowledging the hurt, we can start to get over it. Putting feelings on paper also makes them less intimidating.

Write in your journal during periods of low stress. This will reflect your reality more accurately than in times of high stress, because withdrawal symptoms from cigarette cessation can be as crazed as those arising from a broken romance. They can become so uncomfortable that they may induce you to make excuses, fortifying you to go back to smoking. The journal will bring you back to reality during these times, showing you that your addiction is based more on illusion than on fact.

Try to make an entry into the journal at the end of each day for each practice session. Since your goal is to substitute four or more cigarettes per day, you won't find making journal entries too time consuming.

There are five things to note for each practice session:

- the triggering situation
- the severity of the craving
- the duration of the craving

- which substitute(s) you used
- your satisfaction level after the practice session, and how long it lasted

When rating the severity of the craving, use a scale of one to five, with one being lowest and five being the most severe. Note how long the craving lasted—in most cases a few seconds. If you give in to a trigger, note the amount of time that elapsed before you succumbed to the trigger. Under "Satisfaction," write what made you feel good about not smoking in that situation. If the session was unsuccessful, note how long you felt good about smoking that cigarette and why.

Your journal will show you several things. It will help you gain an understanding of the most effective substitutes for each kind of trigger. If the cravings last a long time, you might want to prepare yourself for future cravings with an extra substitute or two. You will also see that your cravings are temporary and usually pass quickly. For unsuccessful practice sessions please recognize the fact that, although the first drag might have been quite satisfying, you quickly exchanged that satisfaction for regret and remorse.

Review your entries for the day. Give yourself credit for all of your successes and failures of the day, and note what you need to work on.

Your journal will make your break with cigarettes easier. You will get to the point where you will wonder why you thought you couldn't live without cigarettes in the first place.

checklist

✓ Act "as if" you were a nonsmoker for all your practice sessions.

✓ Visualize your success in using substitutes for your practice sessions.

✓ Whenever you have a craving, remember your visualization of the new nonsmoking you.

✓ Whenever you have a craving, switch the dark picture of the smoker you with the light picture of the nonsmoker you, and use thought-stopping.

✓ Use Neurolinguistic Programming to anchor feelings of confidence for those times that you have doubts about your ability to quit.

✓ Choose a buddy to be there for you when you quit.

✓ Choose a role model who doesn't smoke and observe how they handle stress.

✓ Make an entry into your journal for each of your practice sessions, successful or unsuccessful.

Handling Your Stressors

Smokers usually need some help in handling the stressors that tend to beset us each day. After all, smokers have used cigarettes to anesthetize themselves against pain.

You may not be directly able to control your feelings, but you can control your thoughts. You can hang on to a negative thought and replay it; you can reexamine it in a more positive manner; or you can throw it out and replace it entirely.

A negative thought will pass, just like any other feeling, unless we hang on to it. The thing to do is to wait them out, to give them as little attention as possible, and to try to reroute your thinking to healthier thoughts.

Use the suggestions in this chapter to deal with stressful thoughts and situations for the rest of the program. If you want to change something about yourself, finding a role model and acting "as if" are two powerful tools. Now is the time to experiment with, and perhaps change, your whole life!

STRESSFUL EMOTIONS

The helpful hints that follow should prepare you sufficiently to enable you to cope with your emotions by yourself, without any help from cigarettes.

Irrational Thoughts

We reportedly have about 60,000 thoughts a day, 90 percent of which are the same as those we had yesterday. Seventy-nine percent of our thoughts are thought to be negative.

Although any event can usually be looked at from at least two sides, many people tend to adopt one view, often negative. This tendency can conceivably protect them from hurt or disappointment. However, it may not be a fair assessment since it is usually not based on the whole story.

Also not based on reality are irrational thought patterns that are spawned more out of habit than from reason.

Following is a list of common patterns of irrational thinking. Since negative thoughts tend to engender more negative thoughts, it would be a good idea to throw out those negative thoughts that don't stem from reason. They can cause undue stress and pain.

Should statements.

Who is to say what should be, since everything means different things to different people? Next time things aren't going as they should, try to change your expectations of people and the world.

It is absolutely necessary for me to have love and approval from my family, friends, and peers.

Although lovely to have, you can survive without love or approval from anyone.

"If Only's."

What is, is, and no amount of wishing is going to change it. Do what you can to change whatever is in your power, and accept what is not within your power.

Exaggerations.

Using exaggerated negative adjectives just makes for a bleaker sense of reality. Also forget statements like, "If I am rejected I will die" or "I can't stand it." These belong in the same family.

All or nothing thinking.

You pick out a single negative detail and dwell on it to the point that your vision of the rest of your reality becomes dark. For example, seeing an episode of rejection as a never-ending pattern of rejection. This type of thinking overlooks the fact that nothing is black or white.

I should do everything perfectly.

A perfect person would know all there is to know in the world. Since no one knows everything about everything, there is no such thing as a perfect person. You can take pride in knowing that you have done your best.

Certain people are evil and should be punished.

Although these people may be behaving in ways that are antisocial and stupid, it is not your responsibility to mete out punishment.

Happiness can be achieved by being rich and having endless leisure time.

Many studies have shown that the amount of money people have is not a barometer of how happy they are or how much they enjoy life. The culprits for these thought patterns are often black-and-white thinking, overgeneralizing, catastrophizing, discounting positive experiences, and jumping to conclusions.

To get out of this habit, try to take each negative thought that comes up, and ask yourself:

- Is there any rational support for this idea?
- What evidence exists that this idea is false?
- What evidence exists that this idea is true?
- Is it to my advantage to ignore this idea?

- Is it really as bad as it seems?
- What is the worst thing that could happen if I ignore this idea? Can I handle it?
- What alternative ways are there to look at this situation?
- What alternative emotions could I have?

Then follow the negative thought with three positive ones.

Listen to the negative chatter in your mind. Is it based on facts or on old beliefs? Try truly to understand what is going on. Don't magnify the seriousness of a situation with irrational thoughts.

Anger

Anger serves a purpose. It is never wrong to be angry, although problems may occur when you express anger inappropriately.

If you see other people or situations as the cause of your anger, you will always have problems with anger. Remember, *you* decide how you feel.

Next time you get angry, take time out and ask yourself these questions:

- Why exactly am I angry?
- What do I want to accomplish?
- Will my anger help me do this?
- Have these reactions worked in my favor in the past?

If you are angry at someone in particular, ask yourself further:

- Did this person mean to hurt me, or was s/he simply acting in her/his own best interests, without really thinking about how it would affect me?
- What are some of the nice things this person did gratuitously for me?

Acknowledge that you are hurt. Anger doesn't usually change others, and blowing up can be far more damaging than keeping your cool. You can cry, punch something that doesn't cost anything, put it into words on paper, or do nothing and allow it to dissipate.

Expect people to operate more in their own best interests than yours. It is their responsibility to themselves, just as it is your responsibility to first look out for yourself.

If you feel you need to confront the person, tell them how you feel using "I feel" statements, listen to the response, and then try to forgive them. Being able to forgive is one of the characteristics of happy people. It does not mean you approve of their actions, but it does help you by releasing anger and hostility. If you can't forgive, try to at least put it out of your mind, for your sake.

You should also forgive yourself if you are suffering from guilt. Whatever you did, you most likely did the best you could, based on the knowledge available to you at the time. No one is all good or all bad. You choose which part will dominate. You should never confuse what you did with who you are.

Many of us have a lot of anger and unhappiness simply because it is a pattern. If you are chronically unhappy or angry, but you don't believe you are clinically depressed, you may want to read *Feeling Good Handbook* by David Burns, M.D., while you are in this program.

Not asserting yourself can lead to a lot of frustration and anger. You have certain rights in life, and it is up to you to secure them. You have the right to:

- say no without feeling guilty
- ask for things you want
- be yourself, whatever that may be
- make your own choices
- express and have your feelings and opinions
- be listened to
- be treated with respect
- set your own priorities
- be happy

Having these rights doesn't necessarily mean you deserve them. You have to earn them by respecting yourself enough to conduct yourself within the boundaries of your own best interests.

Looking out for yourself is normal and natural, but don't trample over other people in the process. Assertiveness is very different from hostility and aggression. Being equal is different from being overwhelming.

Saying no might seem difficult or awkward at first, but with some practice you will be able to say no with ease and grace, without offending anyone.

Practice saying no to telemarketers, for instance. If someone asks you to do something you really don't want to do, try, "I'd like to but I have to do...." If it's convenient for you (and you feel like it), offer to help to a lesser extent.

Learn to ask for what you want. Rehearse asking if you need to, or write down what you want to say. Know exactly what you want and what compromises you will settle for.

You don't need to cultivate approval from others in order to feel good about yourself. Just be true to your own values.

Disappointment

Disappointment can be very helpful, because at least you know that a particular path isn't going to work. Don't allow any irrational or self-pitying thoughts to exacerbate your disappointment. Remember, you can survive it. Wait out the feelings; they will disappear.

Disappointment teaches you to be realistic about what the future can bring. Expect some disappointment. Discover why you didn't get what you wanted. Did you expect too much?

Expectations, whether they are met or unmet, draw our attentions away from other, sometimes more important, perceptions. Expectations can limit as well as enhance your experience. Don't elevate them to the level of being something you can't live without. Let go of them when they are no longer feasible. Few are matters of life and death. No single outcome is essential.

Worry

Although everyone worries at one time or another, worry is the biggest waste of time. It is normal to anticipate what a potentially painful event might bring, but to obsess over it does no one any good. How often have you pictured how something was going to turn out and seen it turn out differently? By worrying, you pay twice.

No amount of worrying is going to change the inevitable, but there are a few things you can do to alleviate your fears. Ask yourself:

- Does most of what I worry about come true?
- Am I controlling the situation by worrying?
- What is the worst that can happen; would I suffer for the rest of my life?
- Can I accept that?
- Can I prevent what I think might happen or at least reduce the potential damage?
- How?

Change your worry into concern and then action. If you can't resolve a problem immediately, put it into a separate compartment in your brain and come back to it later. If you really need to worry about something, schedule five to ten minutes later on in the day to do so, or give yourself permission for a worry session after more information becomes available.

You may not be able to control everything in this world, but if you do what you can to prevent whatever it is you don't want to happen, you will better accept the outcome.

Anxiety

Anxiety is a pretty common malaise in these times, and the more you obsess about ridding yourself of it, the more it has a tendency to stay.

When anxious thoughts or feelings appear, calmly take some deep breaths and do something else, especially if you are having an anxiety session while lying in bed just before waking up. Don't allow these feelings to interrupt your life.

If you suffer from regular episodes of anxiety, be prepared to accept and live with it for the time being. Accept the sweating or the churning stomach. Don't try to control it or induce a normal feeling. But don't make the mistake of thinking that by beginning to accept these feelings they will go away. Your nerves may still be sensitized and need more time to heal.

Try not to be fooled by physical feelings of anxiety. Usually it is only fearful thoughts rather than a physical threat, that are producing fears and anxiety. Sugar and alcohol encourage negative thinking.

If you begin to feel overpowered by your anxious feelings, seek a physician's advice; several medications are available.

Boredom

Boredom will produce powerful triggers, so you need to prepare for these. Sometimes when you feel depressed or sad, you might simply be bored. Go ahead and feel bored. If you define your feelings more accurately, you will deal with them more effectively. When boredom threatens to trigger a cigarette, use a substitute for Stimulation and Handling Cigarettes and make sure you do something—anything.

Pleasant Emotions

Yes, even pleasant emotions can trigger a desire for a cigarette. Instead of lighting up, focus on the feelings you get from watching a sunset or writing articulately. Bask in these feelings. Use all your senses to enjoy them. Replay them, get excited, make them last as long as possible.

People often think they will be happy when this or that happens. Don't put your happiness on hold. Whether it is acquiring a new outfit or a new car, the happiness you derive from it will be fleeting, and you will soon just want something else. That's why trying to acquire happiness through external means doesn't work.

Happiness is not a constant state but a series of happy moments. Try to fill your life with as many of these moments as possible, and you will find yourself enjoying life much more. The happier you are, the better you will be able to cope with the negative stressors of life, including coping with the loss of cigarettes.

STRESSFUL SITUATIONS

There are many aspects to life—mental, physical, emotional, sexual, financial, social, spiritual, and recreational. Since it is very rare to find them all running smoothly, it is wise to make the best of what *is* working and undertake to fix or accept the rest. If you wait for perfection, you might end up wasting the rest of your life.

Suggestions for fixing up some of the parts of your life that may be causing you stress follow.

Weight Gain

Most people fear gaining weight once they quit smoking, and studies have shown that people do tend to gain an average of three to six pounds. But you don't have to gain *any* weight provided you keep your fat grams and calorie intake down and increase your exercise.

No more than 30 percent of calories should come from fat. Women usually lose weight reducing their fat intake to twenty to forty grams per day and men with thirty to fifty.

Try eating more slowly to give your stomach a chance to fill up. That full feeling takes about twenty minutes to catch up with the food you eat. Also, take sips of water between bites to help fill your stomach more quickly during meals.

Since smoking raises your metabolism, you need more cardiovascular exercise when you stop smoking.

If you are overweight now, try to accept yourself as you are. Promote a more positive body image. Don't say negative things about your appearance when you see yourself in the mirror. Don't compare yourself to anyone else. No one has your unique combination of qualities, so it is an unfair comparison. There are many men and women who are looking for a nice, positive person to be their friend or romantic partner. You don't have to look like a "Barbie" or "Ken" doll to interest these people.

Regardless of whether you gain a few pounds or not, if you keep your fat grams down and do some cardiovascular exercise, it will be far easier to lose the weight than it will be to quit smoking.

Sleeplessness

Problems can become magnified when we are tense or tired. The quality of life also suffers when you are sleepy all the time.

The need for sleep can change throughout a lifetime. If you find yourself tired much of the time, maybe you need more sleep. Try going to bed sooner. Or you may be sleeping too much, in which case, try getting up earlier. Try eye shades or ear plugs to help you stay asleep.

If you are having trouble getting to sleep, take slow deep breaths and tell yourself there is no place you have to go and no problems you have to solve right now. Relax your body from head to toe and, counting down from ten to one, see yourself in your favorite setting. Try natural tranquilizers such as chamomile tea, a bit of warm milk, or sex. Exercising regularly also helps people sleep better, but don't exercise right before bed.

If you are having problems sleeping and nothing seems to work, seek a physician's advice. Many good sleep medications are non-addictive.

Once you quit smoking, you might have interrupted sleep patterns, so expect that you may have to deal with this.

Time

The joy in everyday living is lost when we rush through every experience and ignore the present moment. Be more realistic about your time. Estimate how much time it will take you to do something and then allow ten extra minutes. Do this whether you are finishing a report or going to an appointment.

Don't say yes too much, because you will be overwhelmed. Try to delegate what you can and monitor the outcome.

Arrange your work into two piles, one that must be done now and one that can be done later.

Use the telephone judiciously. It can waste your time as well as save you time. Coordinate telephone calls with mindless tasks you can do at the same time. This can save you a great deal of time.

Get rid of the clutter in your life. Try to keep everything organized so you don't have to rush around looking for things. There is an old German saying, "Those who are too organized, are merely too lazy to look."

Get rid of the clutter in your mind. Know what you want to accomplish in life and you will know your priorities. Buy yourself an organizer and write down even the little things that you want or need to do. Then do the most important things first, and reschedule the rest for the next, or another, day.

No matter how busy you are, take a minute to slow down your pace. Take a lunch break, even if it is short. When you stop at a red light, take a minute to pay attention to the scenery. Take moments regularly to absorb as much pleasure as possible from wherever you happen to be, whatever you happen to be doing. Do this especially with an unpleasant task.

The Past

There is possibly nothing that can sabotage your present and thus your future more than allowing the past to interfere. The past has no business limiting your present, consisting as it does of mere memories. The present is right here, right now. You can use the past as a guide sometimes, but don't give it too much power to influence either your outlook or decisions.

Childhood experiences do not have to dictate how you handle life as an adult. The more you talk and worry about a painful past, the more difficult it is to leave it behind. What causes a problem often has nothing to do with what can solve it. Don't let your childhood ruin you.

Also, don't let a single event color your entire viewpoint on things. Take relationships, for example. There are so many variables in life that there is no way you can predict what is going to happen based on the past, no matter how many similarities exist between the past and present circumstances. The past is often irrelevant.

Don't feel guilty about decisions you may have made or deeds you may have done in the past. You can make decisions only based on the information you had available to you at that time. Everyone makes mistakes, and no one is all good or all bad. You should never confuse what you did with who you are.

Relationships

In this section we will concentrate on helping you achieve as much harmony as possible in your relationships so as to minimize stress.

The five qualities happy families have are love, appreciation for each other, open communication, a willingness to spend time together, and strong leadership. Only relationships that honor feelings build closeness and love. If you do not let others know what you prefer or dislike, you are asking them to read your mind. Most of us are not psychic.

If there is a recurring conflict, let it surface, unexplosively. Often, the longer a conflict is not discussed, the bigger the wedge it can drive between people. It may also keep popping up in different forms. Working out difficulties also tends to bring people closer together.

There are effective and ineffective ways to resolve conflict. Blaming someone, being sarcastic, pouting, withdrawing, abusive language, aggressive yelling and screaming, breaking objects, are not productive and can destroy a relationship.

Don't use accusatory statements like "You never let me finish what I'm saying." Avoid using "always" and "never." Don't preface your complaint with something ominous sounding, such as "There is something I have always wanted to tell you" or "We need to talk." Such statements immediately put the other person on the defensive, making them less open to what you have to say.

If you are asking someone to change, you will be more persuasive if you give supporting evidence for your opinions rather than merely stating them. Make the benefits of changing clear to the other person. If they don't feel the need to change, it is up to you to decide whether you want to continue to deal with that person.

When someone criticizes you, consider what is being said. If there is truth in it, try to fix the problem and thank the person for pointing it out. If you see destructive patterns in your relationships, you might take a look at where your responsibility lies.

Try to communicate on the other person's level. Men and women have different communication styles. Women connect by talking about personal feelings, they like to reveal intimate thoughts, they tend to analyze relationships more than men. Men generally are not as satisfied as women are from just talking. They prefer to act or just to be with someone. They derive feelings of closeness by doing things together. They may show their feelings more by doing something, either directly or indirectly, for their partners, rather than talking.

Friendships and romantic relationships count among the greatest treasures in life. To have a friend, you have to be a friend.

Other Situations

To deal with predictable stress, start by listing the most stressful situations in order of increasing pain—the ones that cause the most turmoil in your life. Then take the situation that produces the least amount of stress. Relaxing yourself first, visualize it, using the technique outlined on page 51. Then visualize yourself handling the situation by using thoughts that will help you cope. Progress to visualizing your handling progressively more stressful situations that you are likely to encounter.

If you find yourself in a stressful situation that you haven't prepared for, before you react, consider the situation objectively. Find the truth of the situation based on the bare facts. Answer any negative thoughts you might have. Catch the stress before it proliferates.

Be careful not to fall into the melodrama trap. If you have a fight with your mate, could you get along with feeling annoyed rather than enraged? Realize also that a difficult morning doesn't mean you have to have a difficult day, any more than having a difficult day means you have to have a difficult week.

checklist

✓ Get into the habit of controlling your feelings by using more appropriate thought patterns.

✓ Whenever an unpleasant emotional situation occurs:
   • Feel each pain without dwelling on it.
   • Read the appropriate section in this chapter to help you cope with it.
   • Use a substitute if you are in a practice session.

✓ If you would like to change in some way, you have two powerful tools: Finding a role model and acting "as if."

Rehearsal Day

Your goal is to go twenty-four hours without smoking.

Pile all your cigarette paraphernalia—cigarette packs (whether full or empty), matches, lighters, and ashtrays—someplace where they will be in full view throughout the day.

Remind your buddy that today is your Rehearsal Day and you want her/him to be there for you. Ask that person to call you later in the day if you think it will help.

Continue forbidding yourself to indulge in everything from the Favorites Sheet.

Follow these steps for cravings:

- Take deep breaths, as many as it takes.
- Use your visualization of the new nonsmoking you.
- Switch dark pictures of the smoker you with light pictures of the nonsmoker you.
- Use thought-stopping.
- Call your buddy.

Don't change your regular routine to avoid cigarette-triggering situations. In fact, seek out and defy as many of them as you can. Do not avoid your smoker friends; instead have them smoke a cigarette in your company. Drink as much coffee as you want, and try drinking a beer or two if that is your habit.

After you successfully complete Rehearsal Day go back to smoking as much as you want except for Mindless Cigarettes, and during practice sessions when dealing with triggers you have not yet confronted three times.

IF YOU ARE HAVING PROBLEMS

If for some reason you feel you absolutely cannot successfully complete Rehearsal Day, go ahead and smoke, but try it again the very next day. This time do not actively seek out smoke-triggering situations. If you feel you can't successfully complete a twenty-four-hour rehearsal period on that day either, go further into the day than the day before by at least thirty minutes, and then try again the very next day. Do not give yourself a day off from quitting. Give it your best shot each day.

If after three attempts, you still can't go an entire twenty-four-hour period without smoking, try these two things for the next two days, in this order:

- Try rapid smoking your last cigarette but only under a physician's guidance.
- Try smoking two in the morning, the last one using rapid smoking, and quit for a twenty-four-hour period from the time of the second cigarette.

Rapid smoking reminds you of the unpleasant effects of smoking that you have trained yourself to tolerate. The average smoker takes a puff every thirty to ninety seconds. In rapid smoking, a large puff is taken every six seconds.

Use rapid smoking only under a physician's supervision. The technique should not be used if you suffer from congestive heart failure or are pregnant.

It will be very helpful for you to get a full twenty-four hours of nonsmoking in before you get to Quit Day. You can console yourself through Rehearsal Day if you need to by remembering that the sooner you successfully complete it, the sooner you will be able to smoke as much as you want guilt-free and basically without constraints until Quit Day.

TROUBLE SPOTS

The day after your successful Rehearsal Day, or during your unsuccessful Rehearsal Days, think back and ask yourself:

- What almost brought you back or did bring you back to smoking?
- How would you like to be able to handle the situation in the future?
- What advice do you have for yourself to combat this on Quit Day?
- If you relapsed, did you feel better after you started smoking again? Did your bad mood get better?

Prepare a written memo to yourself for Quit Day and beyond by answering the above four questions for any potential trouble spots. Then visualize the way you plan to handle these situations in the future.

checklist

✓ Put all your cigarette paraphernalia in a pile somewhere where it will be in full view throughout the day.

✓ Let your buddy know that today is your Rehearsal Day.

✓ Continue withholding from yourself everything from the Favorites Sheet.

✓ Follow the steps for cravings listed in this chapter.

✓ After you complete Rehearsal Day, go back to smoking as much as you want, except for Mindless Cigarettes or during practice sessions for triggers you have not yet confronted three times.

✓ If you feel you cannot complete Rehearsal Day without smoking, try it again the very next day. However, do not seek out smoke-triggering situations.

✓ If you feel you can't successfully complete a twenty-four-hour rehearsal period on the next day either, go further into the day than the day before by at least thirty minutes.

✓ If, after three attempts, you still can't go an entire twenty-four-hour period without smoking:

  • Try rapid smoking your last cigarette—but only under a physician's guidance.
  • If that doesn't work, try smoking two in the morning, the last one using rapid smoking, and quit for a twenty-four-hour period from the time of the second cigarette.

✓ Prepare a memo to yourself regarding trouble spots.

Preparing for Quit Day

Things often go wrong the first week after quitting, due to increased irritation, decreased attention, and sleep disturbances. Expect this and just be happy when things go right. Watch out for self-pity, which could potentially disrupt your resolve. This chapter outlines some things you can do ahead of time to deal with such difficulties.

WITHDRAWAL AGENDA

It is helpful to know the course quitters generally follow so you can be prepared.

Day 1:   Excitement, some withdrawal symptoms.

Days 2–5:   Withdrawal symptoms start to get stronger. You begin to feel like you have suffered a loss and may question quitting. Your emotions may be on a roller coaster from feeling irritable to being excited to feeling depressed.

After that: Life *slowly* returns to normal. Your cravings become less frequent and less intense until they finally vanish.

COPING WITH THE LOSS

You will most likely undergo feelings of loss after you quit. This is normal. Feelings of loss can occur every day, whether it is something major, such as a missed opportunity, or something as minor as a missed telephone call.

Loss typically follows a pattern of stages. However, depending on the perceived severity of the loss, not all stages may exist for all losses. The stages include:

- shock and disbelief
- bargaining, with an offer to change
- grieving, feeling desperate and abandoned
- pain and anguish, feelings of being deprived
- fear, night terror, and sweats
- a fear that you will be alone forever
- sadness and sorrow that your life has led you to this point
- anger or rage at the situation
- depression or feelings that immobilize you
- acceptance and healing, knowing you can survive without it
- hope and rebuilding and taking better care of yourself

With small losses you can go through these stages within minutes, with larger ones it will take longer.

Everyone has losses, but the happiest people are those who can bounce back relatively quickly. You can experience the stages, but you don't have to prolong them by grieving and suffering for too long. Learn to let go. Since you will be getting over it sooner or later, you might as well get over it sooner.

The loss you feel regarding quitting cigarettes will eventually go away. Just as with the loss of any other relationship, be patient and let time take care of it.

TAKING CARE OF BUSINESS

Plan Rewards

For what amount of time would you have to stop smoking in order to believe you could give it up for good? This is your quitting threshold.

What small items have you wanted to buy for yourself but couldn't or wouldn't afford? Buy yourself two gifts—one to give yourself after the first forty-eight hours of quitting. Gift-wrap them if you like. If you don't have the money right now, write yourself an I.O.U. and put it in an envelope to be opened at those times.

What have you really wanted that was too expensive? A vacation? A stereo? Set up a fund for another, bigger, present and try to put in at least half the money you would have ordinarily spent on cigarettes. Put this money in on a daily basis, you'll be more likely to do it this way and it makes your reward seem more tangible. After four months of quitting, give yourself that present.

Stock Up

This is the time to finally stock your refrigerator with the favorite foods and snacks you've been withholding from yourself, as well as the snacks you intend to use as substitutes.

Also stock up on some healthy meals, preferably low-fat and high-fiber foods if you are worried about weight gain. Food can have a powerful effect in fighting the urge to smoke. It is important to eat three well-balanced meals a day, since excessive sugar intake or not enough food will make you irritable, and cigarettes look good to an irritable person. Eating more healthfully also aids in maintaining a constant blood-sugar level, which will help control the urge to smoke, as well as the urge for sweets.

Maintaining your body's energy stores will also help you feel less tired, which will help your body better tolerate stress, as well as curb that empty feeling.

Avoid buying spicy foods, or anything else that may trigger your desire to smoke.

Do buy foods rich in vitamin B$_6$ as well as some tryptophan for your nervous system. Your nerves will probably need all the help they can get. Tryptophan is a naturally occurring enzyme, which the body digests and converts into serotonin. It is good for moods and also aids in concentration. Tryptophan is found in foods high in protein—milk, poultry, meat, fish, and cheese.

Make a Schedule of Fun

Make a schedule for every day of the first week of quitting. Schedule at least one favorite activity per day and as many relaxation periods as you can fit.

Prevent Future Stress

Stress has the greatest potential to seduce you back to cigarettes. Prepare for any stress you can foresee that could jeopardize your determination to quit.

Complete any tasks that cause you stress. Don't make important decisions. Save those for when withdrawal symptoms start to fade. Researchers have found that animals frustrated due to deprivation become hostile and aggressive. Remind family and friends that you will be quitting and warn them that you may be grumpy, very grumpy.

Visit the Doctor

Consult your doctor regarding nicotine replacement therapy, especially if you want to get nicotine nasal spray, Zyban, or Clonidine before your Quit Day, or for guidance on rapid smoking.

It also wouldn't hurt to have your general health checked out even if you don't want any prescriptions. You don't need to have an intense all-day physical, but you could ask your doctor two questions: What do you think about my quitting smoking? Will I gain weight?

Also ask about group therapy or individual counseling offered by hospitals (or the American Cancer Society) as a supplement to this program, if you think it will help.

Visit the Dentist

Get that yellowish or brownish gunk off your teeth with a thorough cleaning. You will be surprised at how much a clean, fresh mouth can influence your desire to want to keep it that way.

THE NIGHT BEFORE

Do not read past this point until the night before Quit Day.

Schedule Fifteen Minutes

Schedule fifteen minutes sometime on the morning of Quit Day to read the "Quit Day" chapter.

Your Last Two Cigarettes

Reserve some private time to enjoy your last two cigarettes. If you realized during Rehearsal Day that you could quit more easily if you had one or two cigarettes in the morning, make sure you reserve enough time for an uninterrupted date with your last two cigarettes on the morning of Quit Day.

Leisurely smoke your second-to-last cigarette and try to pay attention to each puff. Think about why you are quitting, get excited about the rewards you will be seeing, and picture how much better you will feel about yourself and your life. Look at this as an opportunity to finally quit being addicted to the nicotine menace.

Light your last cigarette immediately after you have finished the second-to-last one. Smoke this one rapidly so the cigarette tastes bad. You may feel slightly nauseous or dizzy. Remember this moment with all of your senses. Once you are finished with this cigarette, use some toothpaste if that substitute worked for you.

Remove Paraphernalia

Do a cleanup of all cigarette paraphernalia, including empty packages, matchbooks, matchbook covers, and lighters. Store ashtrays away, out of sight. Throw all cigarettes out unless you are going to smoke one or two cigarettes on the morning of Quit Day.

checklist

✓ Know the quitting agenda so you can prepare yourself.

✓ Buy two small gifts and a big gift as a reward.

✓ Stock your refrigerator with:

- healthy foods, such as fruits, veggies, and bran
- favorite foods you've been withholding from yourself
- your most effective substitutes
- foods containing vitamin B_6 and tryptophan, which are good for your nerves

✓ Make a schedule for every day of the first week of quitting. Plan at least one favorite activity per day and as many relaxation periods as you can fit.

✓ Complete any tasks that have the potential to stress you out for the first week of quitting or that you always smoke while doing and make any decisions that you can now.

✓ Warn family and friends that you will be quitting and that you may be grumpy.

✓ Visit the doctor for any prescriptions you might need.

✓ Visit the dentist to get your teeth cleaned.

✓ Schedule fifteen minutes sometime on Quit Day morning to read the "Quit Day" chapter.

✓ Reserve some private time to leisurely smoke your second-to-last cigarette.

✓ Rapidly smoke the last cigarette, and remember it with all your senses.

✓ Remove any cigarette paraphernalia from sight, clean ashtrays, and throw out all cigarette packs and matchbook covers.

Quit Day

If you are quitting this morning, smoke your last two cigarettes in accordance with the instructions in the last chapter and then read on.

You weren't born with the urge to smoke, and no studies have shown that certain individuals are genetically predisposed toward smoking.

You have a built-in head start when you first quit, because your body has been rejecting cigarette smoke since your very first puff. Since smoking is such an unnatural act, you experienced symptoms such as coughing, dizziness, and nausea, which you had to train your body to get used to. And if you didn't keep practicing, you had to deal with these symptoms all over again. Every time you smoke you are reinforcing the gratification in smoking. But only a few days after quitting, smoking will become more difficult and far less satisfying.

Don't think about never smoking again. Think of giving it your best shot. Just try to get through each part of the day, and don't worry about anything after that. You know you can quit smoking absolutely, since you've been able to quit in most, if not all, the circumstances that prompt you to light up.

Just as with almost any change, quitting may feel rocky or awkward at first and take some getting used to. Once you have adapted to it, you will find it was for the best.

Try to finish reading this chapter this morning.

THE FIRST WEEK

Pamper Yourself

For this first week after quitting, your job is to pamper yourself. If you don't feel like doing something and you can put it off without getting too stressed out later, do it later.

Indulge yourself. Feel free to buy yourself small gifts whenever you want if it won't cause financial problems.

Now you can finally use your favorite foods and drinks, as well as pursue your favorite activities, to combat cravings. If these foods are fatty or not so good for you, phase them out as soon as you think you comfortably can.

Plan some nurturing activities every day or every night, take a hot bath or read a good novel. Follow your schedule of favorite activities and relaxation for the first week.

Don't forget to give yourself your presents after the first forty-eight hours of quitting and after you have passed your quitting threshold. Start your fund for your four-month present, using at least half of the money you would have spent on cigarettes a day.

Your Feelings

Be irritable if you want to and don't feel bad about it. You will probably experience a host of other feelings this first week, most of them unpleasant. Let them come and go and don't give them too much credibility. Do not try to analyze or talk yourself out of them. Although you may miss cigarettes now and sometimes feel that you can't live without them, remember feelings aren't accurate when they originate during duress. Duress in this case comes from missing someone (your deadly white pals) and probably feeling alone.

Being emotional is a normal part of stopping any addiction. Pout intensely, stomp up and down, punch a pillow. Crying relieves tension and restores balance to the central nervous system. We wouldn't have come equipped with tear ducts if we weren't meant to use them. And tests on the chemical composition of tears conclude that tears wept in sorrow have a different chemical composition than those cried over onions. So if you need to cry, cry hard—you'll feel much better for it.

Your Thoughts

Since the physical withdrawal symptoms go away in forty-eight to seventy-two hours, your most nagging triggers will be thoughts. Don't let yourself dwell on the "good ol' days" when you used to smoke. Remind yourself that the cravings are causing your irrational thoughts and that the cravings and the thoughts that accompany them, will eventually go away. And the longer you don't give in, the sooner they will go away.

When Cravings Hit

Follow these steps for all cravings:

- Take deep breaths.
- Pull in your visualization of the new nonsmoking you.
- Switch dark pictures of the smoker you with light pictures of the nonsmoker you.
- Use thought-stopping.
- Call your buddy.
- Read your Quit Sheet.
- Do something from the Favorites Sheet.
- Read your journal entries.

- Tell yourself you can have a cigarette in five minutes. If, in five minutes, you still want to smoke, make yourself wait another five minutes, and then have one if you absolutely must.

Avoid Triggering Situations

For the first five to seven days, try to avoid your strongest triggers, such as alcohol, smoking friends, or anything else.

If you can't avoid a triggering situation, change your routine. For example, take a walk or brush your teeth after your meal or stand while you talk on the phone and keep your calls very short.

Spend time in places you can't smoke, such as the library, a fitness center, or a restaurant.

Water Again

You can help flush out the nicotine and other toxins and cleanse your body by drinking lots of fluids, especially water. Try to avoid any fluids that trigger your urge to smoke, such as coffee, tea, and alcohol.

Sleep

Go to bed early for a while and try to get a full night's sleep. Sleep will also be good for your nerves. But do not use sleeping pills to try to sleep through the initial days of quitting. Sleeping pills won't work, because you need to accumulate experience overcoming triggering situations; you can't do that if you aren't awake.

Use Humor

This is a good time to pull out your humor library. Try to find as much as you can to laugh at, including the fact that you let yourself become dominated by cigarettes. Any laughter you can muster will help to ease your burden.

Give Yourself a Pep Talk

Be proud of yourself. Quitting is one of the hardest things you can accomplish; if you can do this, you can do pretty much anything.

Take your power back! Get mad! Are you going to let a shriveled-up weed control your life? Shape your destiny? Determine how long you live? Do you deserve to be miserable? There are a million successful quitters a year—what have they got that you haven't?

How would a person who doesn't smoke handle the situation? Is this person stronger than you? Smarter? A better person? Look at people around you. Are they really more courageous than you are?

IF YOU REALLY DON'T THINK YOU CAN QUIT THIS TIME

Go ahead and smoke if you feel you really must. It's your body and you can do whatever you want with it, including poison it. But keep in mind that some times are going to be harder than others in trying to handle withdrawals, and you may do much better tomorrow or two days after tomorrow if you can just hold on and not give in right now.

If you really don't want to quit this time, make yourself go through the following steps before you smoke that cigarette:

- Tell yourself to wait just five more minutes and take some deep breaths. If, after five minutes, you still want that cigarette, go to the next step.
- Read your Quit Sheet and take some more deep breaths. Don't just read down the list mechanically, really think about each phrase.
- Remind yourself that you once felt normal and healthy without cigarettes.

- Remind yourself that of course you are going to have some reservations. If cigarettes didn't serve some purpose, you wouldn't be smoking them in the first place.
- Read your journal entries.
- Consider visiting a cancer ward. Seventy to eighty percent of all cancer in the United States is found among cigarette smokers.
- Picture having a cough that won't go away, going to the doctor and being informed that you have cancer. Picture being scheduled for emergency surgery. Picture the surgery not being successful. Would you be able to say it was worth it?
- Ask yourself if your reasons for continuing to smoke are more important than facing the possibility of an early, and perhaps gruesome, death.
- Ask yourself:
  - Why do I want to resume the habit?
  - What am I missing or losing without it?
  - How am I harming myself by giving it up?
  - Do I miss smoking more than I appreciated it?
  - Do I really want to put myself through quitting again?

If you still feel like smoking, make yourself wait five minutes more before you finally light up.

It is a major decision to bomb out on a program after you have invested so much of your time and energy into it, so give some thought to starting to smoke again. There is really nothing positive or productive you can do by smoking even one cigarette. The relief you will get from taking that first puff will quickly mutate into feelings of disgust, regret, and self-reproach. Smoking won't make anything better, but it can make a whole lot of things worse. The temporary discomfort you are now enduring will be worth the permanent benefits.

Although cravings may continue to appear occasionally long after you quit, especially when a trigger comes along that you haven't yet experienced as a nonsmoker, once you have successfully overcome the new trigger you will rarely have to worry about it again.

If you honestly believe that your life is better with cigarettes regardless of the negatives and you won't regret starting up again, go ahead and smoke. You can always quit again later. But if cigarettes really weren't so bad, why did you bother with this program in the first place?

ME—NOW

After all the crying, discomfort, and depression, was it worth it?

Yes! I like no longer having anxiety about the possibility of inducing cancer. I like no longer feeling self-conscious when people groaned and griped about my smoking. I like experiencing the world more directly rather than through a fog of smoke. I like being free to come and go as I please, without having to worry about whether I have cigarettes or the money to buy them before I leave the house.

Quitting smoking was one of the most difficult things I have ever done, and quitting smoking turned me into a much stronger, more confident person. I feel I can do anything now.

Would I do it all over again?

In a minute.

Do I miss them?

Sometimes.

I really enjoyed smoking and loved the taste. And although I still get an occasional craving when I see someone smoking, it lasts less than a half a minute, and then I don't get another one for sometimes months. I can handle that.

I know I could start back up again any time I want, but the benefits of not smoking far outweigh the momentary pleasure I would derive from taking those first few puffs.

checklist

✓ Pamper and indulge yourself the first week. Procrastinate if you don't feel like doing something.

✓ Try to do something nurturing every day. Follow your schedule of fun.

✓ Let unpleasant feelings come and go and try to ignore them. Do not try to analyze or talk yourself out of them.

✓ Get as emotional (in nondestructive ways) as you want to. It will be good for you.

✓ Don't give negative thoughts about quitting too much credibility.

✓ Switch the dark pictures of the smoker you with light pictures of the nonsmoker you.

✓ Follow the steps for cravings:
  • Take deep breaths.
  • Switch dark pictures of the smoker you with light pictures of the nonsmoker you.
  • Pull in your visualization of the new nonsmoking you.
  • Use thought-stopping.
  • Call your buddy.
  • Read your Quit Sheet.
  • Do something from the Favorites Sheet.
  • Read your journal entries.
  • Tell yourself you can have one in five minutes if you absolutely must.

✓ Avoid any triggering situations, and change your routine to do so.

✓ Spend time in places you can't smoke.

✓ Flush out nicotine and other toxins by drinking lots of water.

✓ Get a full night's sleep.

✓ Find as much humor in your life as you can.

✓ Give yourself a pep talk.

✓ Don't forget to give yourself your presents.

✓ Begin the fund for your four-month present.

Maintenance

Studies of the brain's chemistry show nicotine boosts the production of dopamine, one of the brain's natural "uppers." Three-fourths of all relapses take place within three months of quitting, so this effect might explain that high relapse rate—it may take that long just to bring dopamine back up to natural levels after an abrupt drop in nicotine intake.

Remind yourself why you quit every day and appreciate how much closer you are getting to your ideal self. Forget the "just one" idea; puffs are like potato chips—nobody can have just one.

Be prepared to continue to resist your most powerful triggers. In one study 16 percent of all relapsers took their first cigarette with a cup of coffee or tea, and nearly 50 percent when they had been drinking. Alcohol has a tendency to numb that part of the brain responsible for self-control.

If you are gaining weight, eat less fat and more grains, and exercise more. If you do not eat enough, the body goes into a starvation mode and slows your metabolism, so eating less in general won't help you lose weight. It can also make you unhappy, because there's just another thing you can't have that you want.

Don't read the next section unless you relapse.

OOPS

We have already established that there is no such thing as a perfect person. You are not a failure because you didn't succeed in the program, you incurred some degree of success merely because you tried.

A one- or two-cigarette slip-up won't necessarily make you an addict again. People have a tendency to give up if they don't do something perfectly or if they fail. However, each attempt brings you that much closer to your goal, so you should by no means consider it a failure. Instead, consider it a step and think of it as an accomplishment.

If this slip-up turns into a full-blown relapse, it doesn't mean you are a smoker who can't quit. You have merely had a relapse. A relapse is a normal step in the process, since most ex-smokers didn't quit in their first few attempts. Do not reprimand yourself. The only time you fail is if you gave up or didn't even try. Any length of time you can accumulate as a nonsmoker is good because it helps clean out the system.

You may not have enough motivation to quit. You may have to let yourself drift to the bottom first. Find out what caused you to start smoking again and then think of ways to combat it for your next quit attempt.

You may not have been emotionally ready, due to a negative emotional state or chronic stress. You may just need to practice relaxing and learn better coping mechanisms. Or you may need to get rid of whatever is causing that constant influx of stress into your life.

It might be deeper than that. If you are constantly angry or depressed or suffer from other addictions as well, the problem may be more deep-rooted and may require more intensive emotional healing, which therapy might provide.

After how many drags did you lose the satisfaction of smoking? How do you feel now mentally? Are you happy with yourself? Are you reprimanding yourself?

If you are happy with yourself, you might as well continue to smoke until you really want to quit. But remember, cancer doesn't accommodate your schedule: every cigarette you smoke takes five to twenty minutes off your life.

If you are feeling guilty, regretful, and full of self-loathing, try to quit every day until it finally sticks. If you feel you would be better off setting a new Quit Day sometime in the near future (within the next two weeks), go ahead and do that. You merely need more practice. Good luck!

References

Associated Press (London). "Smoking in the Home Tied to More Than Half of Crib Deaths." *Maui News*, July 26, 1996.

Bloomfield, Harold H., Mordfors, Mikael, and Peter McWilliams. *Hypericum and Depression*. Los Angeles: Prelude Press, 1997.

Bloomfield, Harold H. and Peter McWilliams. *How to Heal Depression*. Los Angeles: Prelude Press, 1994.

Blum, Alan. *The Cigarette Underworld*. Secaucus, NJ: Lyle Stuart, Inc., 1985.

Burns, David. *Feeling Good Handbook*, New York: W. Morrow, 1989.

Centers for Disease Control and Prevention (web page): www.cdc.gov/tobacco, September, 1997.

Duke, James. *The Green Pharmacy*. Emmaus, PA: Rodale Press, 1997.

Ellis, Albert and Arthur Lange. *How to Keep People From Pushing Your Buttons*. Secaucus, NJ: Carol Publishing, 1996.

Embree, Mary. *A Woman's Way: The Stop Smoking Book for Women*. Waco, TX: WRS Publishing, 1995.

Ferguson, Tom. *The Smoker's Book of Health*. New York: G.P. Putnam & Sons, 1987.

Fiore, Michael C., et al. "Methods Used to Quit Smoking in the United States: Do Cessation Programs Help?" *Journal of the American Medical Association* (JAMA), May 23/30, 1990.

Glynn, Thomas J. "Methods Used in Smoking Cessation—Finally, Some Answers." JAMA, May 23/30, 1990.

Hiller, M.R. "Many Ways Exist to Stop Smoking." Special to the *Orange County Register*, March 15, 1995.

Keville, Kathi. *Pocket Guide to Aromatherapy*. Freedom, CA: The Crossing Press, 1996.

Padus, Emrika. *The Complete Guide to Your Emotions and Your Health*. Emmaus, PA: Rodale Press, 1992.

Pierce, John P. and Elizabeth Gilpin. "How Long Will Today's New Adolescent Smoker Be Addicted to Cigarettes?" *American Journal of Public Health*, February, 1996.

Report of the Surgeon General. *Preventing Tobacco Use Among Young People*. U.S. Department of Health and Human Services, 1994.

Report of the Surgeon General. *The Health Benefits of Smoking Cessation*. U.S. Department of Health and Human Services, 1990.

Report of the Surgeon General. *The Health Consequences of Involuntary Smoking*. U.S. Department of Health and Human Services, 1986.

Report of the Surgeon General. *The Health Consequences of Using Smokeless Tobacco*. U.S. Department of Health and Human Services, 1986.

Report of the Surgeon General. *Smoking and Health*. U.S. Department of Health and Human Services, 1979.

Stephenson, Joan. "Clues Found to Tobacco Addiction." JAMA, May 24, 1996.

Ulene, Art. *Quit Smoking Today* (videotape). National Broadcasting Company, Inc. and ACOR Programs, Inc., 1995.

Waal-Manning, H.J. and E.A. deHamel. "Smoking Habits and Psychometric Scores: A Community Study." *New Zealand Medical Journal*, September 13, 1978.

BOOKS BY THE CROSSING PRESS

Vital Information Series

Hospitals

By Diane Barnet, R.N.

Hospitals can be intimidating places. Many consumers don't know how to obtain information or even what questions to ask. Hospitals provides inside information for patients and their advocates, and will help you deal with hospitals as a well-informed consumer.

$11.95 • Paper • ISBN 0-89594-908-3

Perimenopause

By Bernard Cortese, M.D.

Perimenopause if the word that refers to the transitional time before and after menopause. This book describes the changes that may take place, discusses the pros and cons of hormone replacement therapy (HRT), offers alternative treatments, and stresses the importance of exercise, proper diet, and stress management.

$11.95 • Paper • ISBN 0-89594-914-8

Surgery

By Molly Shapiro, M.S.N., R.N.

Surgery covers every aspect of the surgery process including what your rights are as a patient. It tells you how to prepare for surgery, what happens in surgery, explains equipment use and procedures, and answers your post-op concerns.

$11.95 • Paper • ISBN 0-89594-898-2

BOOKS BY THE CROSSING PRESS

Making Stress Work for You

By Helen Graham

In this accessible guide, psychologist Helen Graham highlights the positive as well as the negative aspects of stress, showing us how we can reclaim our lives by balancing the energetic forces that influence our behavior.

$14.95 • Paper • ISBN 0-89594-948-2

Pocket Guide to Self Hypnosis

By Adam Burke, Ph. D.

Self-hypnosis and imagery are powerful tools that activate a very creative quality of mind. By following the methods provided, you can begin to make progress on your goals and feel more in control of your life and destiny.

$6.95 • Paper • ISBN 0-89594-824-9

Pocket Guide to the 12-Steps

By Kathleen S.

A time-proven process of healing, the 12-step method is a practical approach to overcoming addictions, co-dependency and compulsions. These steps will help you to heal your relationships with others, master new skills, restore joy and meaning to your life and build a clear sense of purpose.

$6.95 • Paper • ISBN 0-89594-864-8

Pocket Guide to Visualization

By Helen Graham

Visualization is imagining; producing mental images that come to mind as pictures we can see. These pictures can help you relax, assess and manage stress, improve self-awareness, alleviate disease and manage pain.

$6.95 • Paper • ISBN 0-89594-885-0

To receive a current catalog from The Crossing Press
please call toll-free, 800-777-1048.
Visit our Web site on the Internet: www. crossingpress.com